American Made

VOLUME I

*A Prophetic Christian Epistolary Critique
of Modern American Christianity and Culture*

By

JOHN ANDERSON

Copyright © 2026 John Anderson
All rights reserved. Second Edition.

Scripture quotations are from the ESV® Bible (The Holy Bible, English Standard Version®), © 2001 by Crossway, a publishing ministry of Good News Publishers. ESV Text Edition: 2025. The ESV text may not be quoted in any publication made available to the public by a Creative Commons license. The ESV may not be translated in whole or in part into any other language. Used by permission. All rights reserved.

Scripture quotations marked "KJV" are from the King James Version, public domain.

This work is a theological critique. All evaluative statements regarding religious movements, denominations, or systems reflect the author's sincerely held religious beliefs and interpretations of Scripture. References to religious organizations are made solely for doctrinal analysis and theological comparison. The author affirms that individuals within any religious system may hold sincere faith in Christ regardless of institutional structure.

No part of this book may be reproduced, stored in a retrieval system, or transmitted in any form or by any means, electronic, mechanical, photocopying, recording, scanning, or otherwise, without the prior written consent of the author, except for the use of brief quotations in a book review.

To request permissions, contact
andersonbookworks@gmail.com

Paperback: 979-8-9988492-9-9
Hardback: 979-8-9988492-8-2
E-Book: 979-8-9988492-7-5

Printed and bound in the USA
Book design by Kexa

To the entirely lost, those in between, and those who are saved—

The Master calls.

Author's Note

American Made: Volume II is a critical examination of William Branham's Message and high-demand religions. It was particularly relevant in the context of America. After finishing that text, it dawned upon me that the first volume of that series was written just as I had come out of the cult. Though some of my Branhamisms had been successfully weeded out, there was quite a lot that I knew was going to bleed through the cracks. Before long, it became apparent that I should go back and adjust the first volume to align with appropriate theology and my current views, and to make it the definitive edition of the series while retaining as much of that original younger voice as possible. This was my primary motivation when I thought of those in the religions that the second book had gotten them out of, and how they might be tempted to see the first in the series, which could result in some interesting counterproductivity.

That said, in a world as divisive as ours, it would be foolish of me to believe that what is written within this text would be unanimously accepted as truthful, helpful, or loving. I find it worth my time and yours to clarify that these are intended to be as they were titled initially: *Letters of Love*. Love takes on many characteristics in its infinite form, one of which is corrective, and seeing the state of the American-made Church as it is, I believe texts like this are essential to ensuring we correct course before it's too late.

As a believer, it would be disingenuous of me to see the church in the state it's in today and not write in hopes of exposing the many traps, illusions, and mistreatments that the devil has incorporated into our faith. I pray you read this in its intended spirit of love that, though contentious at times, ultimately aims to contend for your soul, battling not against the persons but the principalities.

With all encouragement for critical thinking and the guidance of the open heart, I pray this helps.

~ *John Anderson*

Table Of Contents

Faith Without the Works	13
God's Economy	23
Hate of the World	29
Have Not I Commanded Thee?	35
Generation of Vipers	41
Peace Be Unto You	47
World of the Wicked	53
Curse of the New Year	59
The Blind Believer	65
He Who Makes God Cry	73
The Doctrine of Doom	79
Spirit of the Grieved	87
I See the Storm	93
An Address to the Pope	99
The Importance of the Church	107
The Good Man Wins	113
The Expected End	119
The Clause of Nuclear Hopelessness	127
Generation of Fools	133
The Importance of the Holy Ghost	141
A Word Unto Men	149
Eden's Consequence	157
Nation of Sex	165
Apologetics	173
Whom Shall Be Saved	181

"Those whom I love, I reprove and discipline, so be zealous and repent. Behold, I stand at the door and knock. If anyone hears my voice and opens the door, I will come in to him and eat with him, and he with me."

— *Revelation 3:19-20 (ESV)*

Faith Without the Works

𝓕aith is what we hope for; the evidence of what we do not see (Hebrews 11:1). It is the foundational justification that produces our religion; though we are instructed not to become legalistic, hypocritical, and proud — a fear-based fanatic, we are practitioners of our persuasion, having tangible effects:

> If anyone thinks he is religious and does not bridle his tongue but deceives his heart, this person's religion is worthless. Religion that is pure and undefiled before God the Father is this: to visit orphans and widows in their affliction, and to keep oneself unstained from the world.
> — James 1:26-27 (English Standard Version)

It is essential, primary, and categorically separate from the vindication thereof. It is one of the many things that, if you abound, make you not be barren or unfruitful in the knowledge of the Lord Jesus Christ. The fruit sprouts *after*, not before; *upon* your faith does the seed take root in the fertile ground.

Justification = sanctification + vindication.

Faith is essential. Without faith, we are without God.

For as the body apart from the spirit is dead,
so also faith apart from works is dead.
— James 2:26 (ESV)

Most secularists have a problem with this concept of faith. They call it a "scam," "fake," and above all, "nonsensical nincompoopery reserved for fools and antagonizers." I find this ironic, given that those who say this are actively playing the role of the antagonist upon this parabolic stage before Heaven. They are the faithless, the true antagonists, but not the only ones in the story. Even the occasional Christian joins them, falling under the same title, definition, and judgment.

In a traditional story, the antagonist is the villain. They pose challenges for the protagonist, constantly getting in their way so the protagonist can overcome them and defeat the enemy, teaching us, the audience, a moral lesson. In today's metaphor, the antagonist is the Devil. The protagonist, God, lives within us, and we in Him, meaning Christ — God is the protagonist, and we are made protagonists through him, not of equal value but of imparted righteousness. For clarity, we are not the Hero of the story, but those who benefit from the Hero's work and do heroic things by His heroism. On the contrary, the antagonist's job, his fruit work, contrasts; they're easy to identify. His work challenges the children of God, seeks to devour the world, and, in imparting trials, proves their faith by allowing them to overcome.

This is the testimony of Christ in us: He who began a good work in us will bring it to completion (Philippians 1:6). In that, we adhere to the blood of the Lamb, the word of our testimony, loving not our lives even if unto death.

What are the fruits by which we know the antagonist? It's essential to know who the enemy is, just as well as he knows us; his spirit is already in the world. It's even more important to learn how he acts, what he does, and who he is, so we know *exactly* how to beat him. This is the spirit of the antichrist, a prime example of evil with scriptural characteristics you can identify:

1. He does not acknowledge Christ's coming or that Christ has already come in the flesh.
2. He denies that Jesus is the Christ and that the Father and the Son are one
3. He is a deceiver, showing signs and wonders and, if possible, deceiving the very elect.

In other words, he is anything contrary to the Word. We must ask ourselves, "What are the fruits of the *protagonist?*" They are the fruits of the Spirit. The children of God are known by their fruits, the same way the antichrist is known by his; only ours come from being aligned with the Scriptures of which our religion is derived. We then return to James, who said, "If you have faith but no works, then your faith is *dead.*"

"Anything contrary to that script is of the devil," most legalists say, to which I agree. Positionally, it is not the question of whether or not works will be present, but how you view your works that is salvifically critical. If we are truly a protagonist, then we shall declare:

"It is according to the testimony of Holy Scripture that we are justified before God by grace through faith alone, not by works of the law. Salvation is the gift of God, not a result of human effort, merit, or righteousness, for if that were true, then Heaven would be filled with boastful people. No, Heaven is filled with that sinner who was declared righteous by his faith in Christ Jesus, making him a sinner no more as he trusts in the finished work, basking in the righteousness of God, a sinner no more.

"Whoever believes in the Son *has* eternal life, *has* passed from death to life, and stands before God justified, glorified, and in peace through our Lord and Savior. This is entirely by His mercy and not our piety. Eternal life is given to all who trust in the One who so loved the world that He gave His only begotten Son, so that whosoever believeth in Him shall not perish but have everlasting life.

"That is the Gospel: simple; sufficient. Believe in the Lord Jesus Christ, and you *will* be saved. Those whom God calls He saves, and those He saves he preserves, and those He preserves He glorifies from the beginning of our salvation to its completion — it is a work that belongs to God. He who began it in His people will finish it, for it has been finished, and does not need any additional sacrifice.

"God is faithful, and those whom He brings into the fellowship of His Son will be sustained to the end, kept blameless in the day of our Lord — those whom He foreknew, predestined and conformed to the image of His Son by the work that originates from His eternal purpose. Therefore, we have peace in knowing that nothing in *all* of creation can separate believers from the love of God in Christ: Not death. Not life. Not angels, rulers, things present or things to come, nor powers or heights and depths.

"Not even ourselves. No believer is stronger than the hand that holds him, and despite his failures, he is not released, for Jesus promised that all whom the Father gives Him will come to Him, and whoever comes is His sheep, shall hear, follow, and not be lost, but raised in the last day. His sheep hear His voice; He knows them; He gives them eternal life, and they will never perish when in the hands of the Father who gave them, being greater than *all*. When this sheep — not dog, pig, or goat, but sheep hears, repents, and believes the gospel, they are sealed with the promised Holy Spirit: the guarantee and payment of our inheritance until we acquire possession of it. This is our mark, the seal that signals those who belong to God and are awaiting the day of their redemption, the day of the return of our blessed hope, Jesus Christ. It is by his crucifixion, burial, and resurrection from the dead, of the dead, that we have been born again to a living, breathing hope — an imperishable inheritance, undefiled and unfading.

"That is what is held in Heaven for us, now and forever. By God's power, we are guarded through the faith of our salvation, ready to be revealed in the end times.

"Christ is our intercessor; we do not need anyone else. He is the Redeemer of His people and can *completely* save those who come to God through Him. By a single offering, He has perfected for all time those who are being sanctified, vindicating the existing faith that they and men might see. The God of Peace is the sanctifier, the provider of evidence to the eternal claim of the perseverance of the saints, keeping them wholly in spirit, soul, and body, blameless at His coming.

"He who calls them is faithful; He will surely do it. Therefore, true believers will persevere because they are kept; those who ultimately depart from the faith have shown that they were never truly His, for if they had been, they would have continued. For by their strength they left or were defeated, but by God's strength we are grounded in His preserving grace. This is His divine work, our possession of assurance, of which Scripture declares is the Good News, that those who believe in the name of the Son of God may know that they *have* eternal life.

"Salvation, from justification to final glorification, is entirely the work of God's grace received through faith, accomplished by Christ, applied by the Spirit, and preserved by the power and faithfulness of God forever."

— A harmonization of the Scriptures on faith alone, justification, salvation, and the perseverance of the saints.

Are you a protagonist or an antagonist? Does your faith live or die? Asking yourself these questions is essential to discovering where we go from here.

Obedience to Christ is the generalized work of the faith, though it is not what saves us. Let it be known that *we* are not salvation. We're nothing more than a vessel used to bring Christ, who *is* salvation, to others, like water in a pot from a well amid a desert. How do we do this? Through God's sovereign distribution and to the stewardship and servitude of the body of Jesus Christ. Whether it be apostles, pastors, prophets, teachers, evangelists, apologists, or other gifts dedicated to the ministry, it is the perfect synchrony that exposes those who thirst for Christ's never-drying well to the water source.

Writing, baking, painting, singing, teaching, loving, befriending, and fellowshipping, among other things, are the gifts we have been given to aid the kingdom. When given to God, *these* gifts are a ministry for the kingdom of Heaven, and when done daily, are what real worship is:

> I appeal to you therefore, brothers, by the mercies of God, to present your bodies as a living sacrifice, holy and acceptable to God, which is your spiritual worship. Do not be conformed to this world, but be transformed by the renewal of your mind, that by testing you may discern what is the will of God, what is good and acceptable and perfect.
> — Romans 12:1-2 (ESV)

Many of us are evangelists and don't even realize it, and we may even have more than this. Alas, you *must* begin working to discover which part of the ministry you are and what you're meant to become — faith alone saves, but saving faith is never alone. That is the line between the protagonist and antagonist; if your faith is dead or alive, having obtained the life that makes the works wonderful.

Suppose we partake in anything contrary to the Word, even in the twisting of it or the miscategorization of justification by faith, then we are the antagonist. Our works are the completion of our justification, meaning it is the vindication, the evidence of what has been made clear to God but is unclear to men. Alas, the antagonist is needed for the protagonist. Even as a force of evil, we can be used for good; it is only a shame to see, given that those who choose antagonism could be protagonists if they made the contrary decision.

The greatest tragedy is reserved for those who call themselves Christians without realizing the role they're playing, for they have deceived themselves into believing they are sinless or that their works are something more than a filthy rag. Imagine how proud the devil is of us when we use our faith as another means to work for him.

Those who are more hypocritical than they are atheists have my pity. They choose to live in misery as an antagonist, tortured by the main one without realizing it. When I see someone like this, I ask myself how they got there, and discover the answer is as simple as the question: it was by their religiousness.

Organized religion — denominations — are more satanic than the satanic temples, it seems, for they are far more divisive, even if in their labels, and have demonized everyone else in their quest for superiority. At least Satanists are honest and open about who they are; that is their foundation. In contrast, the mega-churches, cathedrals, and the cult-shaped lodges produce doctrines of lies, and the leaders are closer to false teachers or wolves in sheep's clothing, seeking whom they may devour, for their money, power, and greed than a proper shepherd.

I am fascinated by the realist, gifted with discernment and the ability to see through the fallacies and deceptions propagated by self-proclaimed representatives of God. Because of this, the average atheist turns their back on God and, even after doing this, has a better opportunity to make it to Heaven than the most religious Christian.

The angry banter and tirade of the atheist is a greater work of faith in "nothing" than the Christian's lack of real, true work despite their belief in "Something."

Christians in their religious shells: you must *break out*. You are in *danger*, not realizing how harmful your dogmas and traditions are, being a servant of Satan in his possession, doing far more damage to yourselves and others than the devil could have ever dreamed. You must break out of your religious chain and enter the yoke of Christ, for it is light and easy, but you have made it a ponderous chain in your Scroogean greed, Christ after Christ and Mass after Mass, unworthily drinking the blood you vampirically gulp. All of us who, by our own works, believe we have put ourselves in Christ's bondage, when we have only doomed ourselves to an eternity of restlessness and turmoil.

Are you written in the Lamb's book of life, or in the mega-churches, prosperity, or your own vainglory? In taking Christ to the faithless and the faithful, we lead them to him, not us. *This* is eternal life. We serve God, not man-made dogma. With this service, we shall do the works in our scriptural time, not defilement, or anything that worketh abomination, such as sin, the wages of death, the disobedience of God, spreading lies like the Luciferian ideology in Genesis, in the Serpent's continuation of evil to destroy mankind.

This is the foundation for these letters, and I hope that by reading them, you can answer the following questions: What are you? Are you a protagonist or an antagonist? Are you working or dying? I pray this helps you answer the question and come alive through the works of Jesus Christ.

God's Economy

I am writing today with a testimony relevant to our current economic situation. As best I can read, these circumstances seem dire: We face an economic recession fueled by indecision. To clarify, in hopes of avoiding the courts and council, this is not financial advice in the literal sense but spiritual counsel to help us with our unseen wealth via the analogous exemplification of modern times.

> For the love of money is a root of all kinds of evils. It is through this craving that some have wandered away from the faith and pierced themselves with many pangs.
> — 1 Timothy 6:10 (ESV)

    It is known that the things of this world, and the evils thereof, do not run rampant without the Lord having taken all of them into subjection and for his many uses. The inspiration for this text comes from economic struggle, which, like all life's issues, is addressed in the Bible. The gospel states that we should not worry about worldly things. The Provider provides food, water, clothing, and funds. Still, as Gentiles, it is our nature to fear the lack thereof because of the associated thoughts plaguing our minds. This can make us not see clearly, like a sailor entrapped amid the fog that flows over the ocean before the lighthouse.

In fairness and humanity, it is understandable to ask how we are not to worry about food when there's more than one mouth to feed. Fair-mindedly, we know that without clothes, we run naked, and without money, all things previous cannot be attained. Alas, there is an opening for the root of all evil to bore itself into our lives. That is where the Suffocate of Freedom can be revealed.

But what of the spiritual perspective?

Currency, as wicked as it can be, has a heavenly catch: in the words of a minister before me, "Money is a terrible master but a marvelous servant." The Earth's economy is an absolute in our lives. It is not in our best interest to change this variable, nor is it possible in an economic world to completely reject it. Instead, we should change the value it's been given — the position of its placement in our lives through God's mathematics. Not only does God provide all things, but he *multiplies* them in His time and season. Whether spiritual or physical, it is the cheerful giver that shall see the glorification of God in a grace-driven act to give:

> The point is this: whoever sows sparingly will also reap sparingly, and whoever sows bountifully will also reap bountifully. Each one must give as he has decided in his heart, not reluctantly or under compulsion, for God loves a cheerful giver. And God is able to make all grace abound to you, so that having all sufficiency in all things at all times, you may abound in every good work.
> — 2 Corinthians 9:6-8 (ESV)

The supplier of seeds to the sower will have his seed for sowing multiplied in righteousness; that which you do on earth shall have rewards in heaven. Investing in God, the Eternal Economist, bears far better fruit in all seasons than the American bill.

God is backed by His standard, booming, and consistently providing the prerequisites for His children. Meanwhile, backed by an invisible, fabricated, and unfaithful bankroll, the dollar could be easily thwarted by no more than a flickering flame of inflation. It is only sensical to place God at the forefront of our lives, and we shall be about the most excellent business, representing and reflecting Christ.

Activate your faith, my brothers and sisters. Be *brave* enough to be a spiritual entrepreneur. Through your faith and understanding of all these things,

you will invest in your spiritual bank and witness God's workings through His promises. No, God is not actualized in the dollar bill alone; He is made real in *all* things if He is the focus of your life. When He is all you look to, He is all you will see. As you continue your walk, He will increase all things, first spiritually.

In your hard work, you will be rewarded. In your wisdom, you shall not be destroyed.

You will be blessed in your charity, the chief of all these things. From this, all believers, in perfect placement, shall witness the compounding of God's economy — His people, valued appreciably more than anything, despite our spiritual and literal recession. Amid regeneration, the economy booms; amid a recession, spending is scarce. Take this in a parabolic sense, so you may be immune to the economic crash soon to come, constantly present but on hold by the hand of God.

Worry not about the things of this world; God sees *you*.

Always pray, my brothers and sisters. Invest in your heavenly home. God will not leave you nor forsake you; this is *certain*. I have seen the hand of God in my life, especially in critical times such as these. He will deliver you and provide for you, despite what we may go through, and He is the only investment worth making.

Hate of the World

    Because of the recent decisions I've made regarding the work that I can do, I have seen the face of hate. I have seen the devil in his unfiltered form and how wicked he and his minions can be. It's no surprise that in the times of the patriarchs and now, they have been slaughtered, imprisoned, tortured, scrutinized, and, above all, hated by the people of this world — Satan's servants. If it were legal, I'm convinced I would be dead already. Even illegal, I feel the target on my back, the laser beams locked as prying eyes watch from the shadows.

    In moments like these, you realize how much the Lord loves you, how much He protects you, and how much love He offers. You also see the spirit of the antichrist and how many people it has under its spell.

    You can see the *hate:*

If the world hates you, know that it has hated me before it hated you. If you were of the world, the world would love you as its own; but because you are not of the world, but I chose you out of the world, therefore the world hates you."
— John 15:18-19 (ESV)

There are occasional Christians who don't like to discuss these hard-hitting topics. The concept of hatred either scares them or is too harsh to handle, so they ignore the matter or sugarcoat the Gospel to avoid scandal. But God does not ask us to sugarcoat His word; He asks us to believe it and *proclaim* it. The word of God is sweetened enough, for the mouth at least, before it turns bitter in the belly. Speak the word of God as He gave it to us, not in the way that the world would like to hear it, for if the world loves it, it is not of God but of the world:

> Remember the word that I said to you: 'A servant is not greater than his master.' If they persecuted me, they will also persecute you. If they kept my word, they will also keep yours.
> — John 15:20 (ESV)

My people get just as frustrated with me as atheists do. From what I have seen, the reason is that most lack the courage this Gospel requires, or they have manipulated it to the point that it is of no effect and is more the Devil's than God's. They do not keep His sayings, spirit, fruits, or works, and instead choose to line their pockets rather than face persecution or choose tradition over the Testimony. This irks them greatly, and I understand this reaction: Paul has said that the Gospel will offend the egomaniacal (Galatians 5:11).

Like Paul, I have found myself entertaining the very same thoughts, especially recently, when thinking about the evangelical approach, given the persecution and punishment I have experienced. I have considered taking the easier way, but how could I live with myself if I were not living for others? We are not greater than God. We will obtain the promises of the Word, both positive and negative. We want the blessings, yet don't want the challenge of being given them. This is a dangerous way of thinking, given that Satan can offer worldly blessings (Matthew 4:8-9) in a counterfeit way to Christ. Arguments can be made that because of its little to no challenge of obtaining, it is far more tempting and accessible. He has offered prosperity and power to the worst of all characters, while God offers a better character, sometimes through poverty and powerlessness.

These are the words the average American doesn't like, that the capitalist tends to reject:

> If I had not come and spoken to them, they would not have been guilty of sin, but now they have no excuse for their sin. Whoever hates me hates my Father also. If I had not done among them the works that no one else did,

they would not be guilty of sin, but now they have seen and hated both me and my Father. But the word that is written in their Law must be fulfilled: 'They hated me without a cause.' "
— John 15:22-25 (ESV)

Some atheists say, "There's no hate like Christian love," which is an ironic saying told in the most hateful spirit by those who claim they bring the "better walk of life." To counter, if our love is hate, I would hate to see your idea of love, for there is no hate like the devil's distaste, repeated by the drones who read from his scripts, known as miserably confused servants.

I don't say this with hatred or anger; it is merely a disheartened observation from my experiences. You grieve me, bother me, as the world does. Oh, how lost it is, how willing you are to spew venom as hypocrites who criticize love while acting as harbingers of evil. These are the same people who then imprisoned the patriarchs and now do the same, unto torture or death.

Though my experience may not be like theirs, as of now, my detainment through censorship of free speech is torturing me with the fact that I cannot speak to the people through one of many avenues the Lord has provided, the number of times I have been criticized, ridiculed, made fun of, and attacked for my looks, my wife, my faith, and above all, the word of God, is not only a *staggering* amount but one that should bring shame to their organization, which is not to say that I am the standard nor the example, but that I am one of many instances representing the bigger picture — that the hatred is *real*.

I ask, "How can these representatives hope to make conversions with this approach? How does it work on so many? How do they fall into this trap? What more can I do to help those who will listen to avoid falling into the jaws of the lion?"

We do what we can with what we've been given. I suppose that's all we can do, for hatred is the expectation when we bear the Good News. We, the predestinated few, who cry out to those who will know His voice, the very same one that made Man in His image. We are humbled in so much that the last will be first, and the first last, which is to say that salvation is by grace, not merit, and that though our fellow man might overlook us, in the eyes of God, we are seen, regardless of status.

In the Kingdom to come, the economy will be reversed, and the earthly possessions and persecutions will be no more. The Spirit of Truth is known by the chosen; He knew and loved them first: Those who have that deep calling to the deep in a world that hates the truth while propagating lies as facts. There is only one truth, one constant, one way, one life, one Word, one God, and his name is Jesus Christ. Paired with that body, within that body, is the Bride of whom the Groom comes for. He is the same yesterday, today, and forever — God made flesh — the living Word who has sent a Helper to live within us as we live in Him:

> But when the Helper comes, whom I will send to you from the Father, the Spirit of truth, who proceeds from the Father, he will bear witness about me.
> — John 15:26 (ESV)

I am motivated by knowing that whomever I cry out to may hear the Voice behind the voice, the Holy Spirit moving within and around us to obtain those who are His by means of the truth among the lies, life in a world of death, grace in a world of law: The Word in a world of the mute.

I am comforted by the thought that there is Love in a world of bitterness, even if only seen in my fellow believers, who are speakers of His Word that we adore.

Have Not I Commanded Thee?

Courage is more easily spoken than practiced. It's easy to talk about what the Lord can do, but it's challenging to put yourself in a position to allow Him to do the things he needs to do with you. We talk about boldness day in and night out, but when a challenge such as terminal illness stares us in the face, suddenly that overwhelming presence of fear kicks in. We speak highly of love yet curse when we're faced with hate. We ask God for a wife and then run when a woman looks our way.

In other words, we have lost our backbone. We, the wicked and adulterous generation of little faith, lack *courage*.

Like God and His people, this world and age require courage. Cowards will not endure until Christ's second coming; only those who were brave enough to stand up against the Devil — the heroes of the faith — who believed and received the Holy Spirit.

The Lord has been working with me on this subject, and it has been a hard lesson to learn. I thought I was a force to be reckoned with until I came face to face with Satan, who used my greatest weaknesses against me. The Devil knows no limits. He fights filthily. We expect the enemy to come from behind enemy lines, but what we least expect is when he comes from friends, family, and loved ones. Add to that his armament of our childhood trauma and the weaponization of our insecurities, and we have ourselves a recipe for disaster.

But with God, there is hope:

> No man shall be able to stand before you all the days of your life. Just as I was with Moses, so I will be with you. I will not leave you or forsake you.
> — Joshua 1:5 (ESV)

Like Joshua, we can examine his character to see the exemplification of a man of boldness and derive such heroic principles from him. We are no longer under this covenant, knowing we do not battle against flesh and blood but principalities, and therefore understand that we do not confuse taking up arms against the vessels of the Devil with the reality that they have taken up arms with the Devil himself. Therefore, our best armament is to do the same:

> Be strong and courageous, for you shall cause this people to inherit the land that I swore to their fathers to give them. Only be strong and very courageous, being careful to do according to all the law that Moses my servant commanded you. Do not turn from it to the right hand or to the left, that you may have good success wherever you go.
> — Joshua 1:6-7 (ESV)

Have strength. Be good. Have courage.

Follow the law, be a servant, prosper in times of blessings, and suffer in times of trial. The God of Joshua of the Old Covenant is our God of the New Covenant. We shall obtain all things as God has willed, giving to us what is in accordance with His will and carrying us through all that is not of ours. We will prosper if we ask in the Spirit of God that He placed in our hearts. *Then* vanity is done away with:

> This Book of the Law shall not depart from your mouth, but you shall meditate on it day and night, so that you may be careful to do according to all that is written in it. For then you will make your way prosperous, and then you will have good success.
> — Joshua 1:8 (ESV)

Do you want to prosper? Be strong and of good courage. Do you want the victory? Follow the Law; be a servant. Having eternal life — the inheritance, Canaan; we should want to do these things, to go into all the world and preach the Gospel so that whosoever hears it will not perish but have everlasting life, being made free indeed while receiving the joy of their salvation as we did before them. We do not go to a lonely land reserved for a few, but the promised land, a home for *multitudes*. It is not mine or yours alone, but *all* of the Bride's safe space.

> Have I not commanded you? Be strong and courageous. Do not be frightened, and do not be dismayed, for the LORD your God is with you wherever you go.
> — Joshua 1:9 (ESV)

Where is she? She's out there where we once were, in the world, waiting for her unknown Bridegroom who will use us for his work if we want to engage in that love. The Word of God is our weapon, not to use against the people but to use against the enemy. Do you want success? Meditate day and night to do all that is written. Do you want to prosper? Remember whom the Commander commands: the good and faithful servant, for our prosperity is not tied up in our materialism, but in the immaterial promise that we have and will see one day.

Who is your commander? Who tells you what to do? Whom do you serve? Have you seen the nature of the serpent or the dove? Are you of God or the Devil?

Who is your master?

If your master is God, then you will be strong and of good courage, for He commandeth you. He leads you through the battle to take you to the promised land. He will not leave you nor forsake you. But Satan? He is a *punishing* and *fear-mongering* master who leads you down the path to damnation, making you feel pain, cowardice, anger, and hatred.

What good has that ever done?

There is no good in it of itself. The only way it can be worked for good is through God. So, we should not be afraid, brotshers and sisters. The Lord thy God is with thee, whithersoever thou goest. Be courageous and well-versed in the word, my fellow fighters; lean not to your understanding. If you do, you will fail and act as a devil-servant. Yet, as a servant of God, you shall not perish but have everlasting life.

Go, my friends, taking Christ with you.

The fight is not yet over.

Generation of Vipers

My spirit is grieved.

As a modern man who walks in the darkest hour, the end of days, I expect such feelings, but that does not make them any less challenging to handle. I know the actions of this generation are prophesied; they who are the Godless, wicked, and adulterous — a generation of vipers.

This implies that they have not always been, but are now due to the corruption of minds and the death of the spirit that have come by politicians and principalities. Both are working together, in bed with one another, as the Mother of Harlots works its power behind its walls. There is a demonic air that plagues the pen that goes to paper when creating the laws and politics that further sink the teeth of the enemy into the people. On both sides, red and blue, we see the jaws of the one who walks about as a roaring lion, seeking whom he may devour, ensnaring the believers and the not in political jargon, conversed first in Hell before being sent to the cell phone. We are headed in one prophetic direction; as God said, this will not change. Still, I feel the need to write to the people in these final hours, praying, hoping, and believing that God will reach you through this gift.

I pray you see my heart and its intentions. I am not arguing your politics; I am fighting for your *soul*. I don't desire to fight you, but the devil within you.

Wake up, my people! If anything, use your reasoning to hear this message: God is still saving; there is still mercy, for now, until it is too late, whose time will be made known by the coming of the Lord. If you genuinely care for the people and are troubled by the circumstances, like anyone with a heart would be, amplify your natural love through the conduit, Christ, for God's love conquers all. His love is eternal. It is non-corruptible, perfect in all ways, and just in all teachings.

Do you want results? Go to God, for if you genuinely love the people, then you are of God, for God is love.

Look not to John, the son of Anders, but look to Christ. If you can see the similarities in the comparisons to the Good Book, then you know it can be trusted. The Word of God is the ultimate truth that is, now, as it was then: *infallible*.

I cry out to you, my people, to pull you from the trap of politics, moralized by the wicked and enforced by the Devil. I see hatred within this system, corrupted by powers we cannot imagine and ruled by men you cannot see. What happened today was planned fifty years ago, and what will happen tomorrow was the same, organized by the men seeking to *steal* it. Still, all the plans these men may make are laughable to God, for His plan is unfolding within and without them. Whether they do it knowingly or not, accept it or not, believe it or not, they are tools in His hands, the same as us. I say this to prove a point: If you have already attained victory through the blood of Jesus Christ, why do you align yourself with those who have not? Why do you align with the lost in mind and soul?

I am tired of the deceptions God's people entertain, so now I declare: *Godless* politics are Satanic politics.

Remove yourself from worldly things and be placed in a perfect position. Align yourself with God's laws, not the laws of man, obeying them, contending for them only to the degree that they do not compromise our faith. The evil that comes forth like a flood seeks to take more than your property, money, and rights; it seeks your inheritance — your salvation — a greater value than all precious metals and dollars the world has to offer combined. It's worth more than all worlds, known and unknown. *You* are the currency the rich and powerful have yet to acquire — those who have sold their souls for the world's kingdoms.

Turn away from them, children of God! Now, not later! Adorn yourselves in modest apparel and the whole armor of God, not the worldly nonsense that the rat race has given value. We are not rats; we are sons and daughters of God.

Though, as Gentiles, we have been parabolically compared to dogs, that does not mean we partake in the dog-eat-dog world. Those who know God have had a change of nature, so we are not the same creature of the metaphor anyhow; if you do not know God and have not been changed, then let the foot of which the boot fits wear it.

Turn away from false prophets, false teachers, and their political alliances before it's too late.

Don't support Israel because you are a Republican, nor Palestine because you are a Democrat; help the people, God's and not, through the eternal revelation that is the Solid Rock, Jesus Christ. Though minuscule, anything else wastes your efforts, and you fall into the political trap planted to sow seeds of hate.

Don't be mistaken, my fellow servants; I grieve for the populace all the same as you. Still, I rest in the finished work of the blood of Jesus Christ to make changes in the people, change where it matters. We should use the Word of God for this, not for the power of spreading hate disguised as virtue, though false, realistically amounting to nothing for the people being talked about, but everything for the one talking about them.

Do you want to stand for Israel? Go to the Lord in prayer. Do you wish to do the same for Palestine? Go to the Lord in prayer. *Prayer* is a great weapon against the spirits at play, and believe not me, but God, when we say we battle against principalities. The lie of the modern political activist, atheist, agnostic, or general non-believer is that prayer is the weakest, nay, most irrelevant action one could take. This is ironic, given that a fervent prayer by a righteous servant works better than a social warrior who yells about the same issues from their self-proclaimed social biographies or in the faces of others, whether or not they are relevant.

There is more progress in working than in speaking about it.

Since when did we decide to stand for countries rather than God? Where do we find the scripture that asks us to put politics before the Lord? Where do we see the scripture that asks us to place politics before our beliefs? You, men of the world, who have *lost* your humanity: You have paired your souls with serpents and have been blinded by their beauty. You, generation of vipers, spewing venom, poisoning all, and flashing your vanity through your false virtue, acting as scales that shield your heart of flesh, the hypocrite who hides inside.

I pray you see my heart and its intentions. I am not arguing your politics; I don't even desire you to quit politics altogether, for that would be unwise and unrealistic; I don't desire to fight you, but the devil who oppresses you; I am fighting for your *soul*.

Wake up, my people! If anything, use your reasoning to hear this message: God is still saving; there is still mercy, for now, until it is too late, whose time will be made known by the coming of the Lord or their timely-untimely death. If you genuinely care for the people and are troubled by the circumstances, as anyone with a heart would be, amplify your natural love through the godly love of Christ, for God's love conquers all. His love is eternal.

If those who are evil can understand the concepts of good in politics, and what good is to be done even in the secularist's view, how much more does our Father who is in heaven know what is good for all? He is non-corruptible, perfect in all ways, and just in all teachings.

If you want results, go to God; if you genuinely love the people, then prove it by bearing the fruits of the Spirit, knowing that God is love.

"O generation of vipers, how can ye, being evil, speak good things? for out of the abundance of the heart the mouth speaketh."
— Matthew 12:34 (King James Version)

Peace Be Unto You

*T*oday is a *good* day.

It's not every day that I write a peaceful address. My prose is heavier more often than not, and I, its penman, must bear the weight of that burden. Still, I happily ask, "What is an ox without a yoke, a fisherman without an ocean of fish, or a writer without a pen?"

Burden-less, I presume.

It is said that the pen is mightier than the sword. I say it *is* the sheath of the Word written in ink and blood, held by the strongest believers, transcribing the Sword that we use to combat heresies and what have you.

To those who bear this weight: peace be unto you.

So many of us get caught up in the weight of God's Word. This is no surprise, given that one cannot simply dive into God's eternal ocean of revelation without feeling like they are drowning. God is many things: deep, overwhelming, infinite, and endless. It is hard to fathom, at times. Occasionally, I feel like no matter how much I do for Him, it will never be enough. No matter how meaningful my life is, it'll never amount to *His*. If you've had this thought, do not give in to the anxiety that it brings and is born from its existentialism, but instead, take the thought and seek the Lord rather than *it,* for though it is true, it is not entirely the point. God is our guide. He leads us through the depths of His word, provides us with revelation, and gives us the strength and knowledge to wield the sword.

> Then the same day at evening, being the first day of the week, when the doors were shut where the disciples were assembled for fear of the Jews, came Jesus and stood in the midst, and saith unto them, "Peace be unto you."
> — John 20:19 (KJV)

After weeks of being held up where Jesus commanded the disciples to go, facing doubt, anxiety, and fear, Jesus arrived with a simple message: peace be unto you. As simple as it was, it bore repeating, for in verse 21, he says, "Peace be unto you: as my Father hath sent me, even so, send I you" (John 20:21, KJV).

Fear is terrible, but depending on its master, it can be used for good or evil. Fear of the devil is domineering and dreadful; it threatens our lives, as the disciples' did. We feel fear and anxiety in many situations, from our jobs to our partners to our everyday comings and goings. For some, that moment in the witching hour when something goes bump in the night is the most fear-filled of all. To that I would ask, "Who is your master?" Fear of the Lord is reverence and respect, understanding His overwhelming love.

If your fear is in Christ, then peace be unto you. We are not given a spirit of fear but of power, love, and a sound mind; perfect love casts out all fear.

In verse 22, the Word says, "And when he had said this, he breathed on them, and saith unto them, receive ye the Holy Ghost" (John 20:22, KJV). The Holy Ghost, the Holy Spirit, is the third person of God. He was the Word made flesh to dwell among us, and He dwells within us, His chosen temple, where He is delighted to dwell. He is that same spirit who bears the same characteristics of a Christian being sanctified in His ministry.

The pastors, teachers, and evangelists of God, all filled with the Holy Ghost, are given the power to overcome the dominators of this world.

Peace be unto you.
Whose soever sins ye remit, they are remitted unto them;
and whose soever sins ye retain, they are retained.
— John 20:23 (KJV).

The disciples, in their moment of fear, are given the commission of the Gospel, the only power able to remit and retain sins, for it is by the work of Christ that all sin is blotted out, not the priesthood that arbitrarily obtains succession. Though we may not be apostles, we understand the peace to be felt in the Gospel of Jesus Christ — we, the sons and daughters of God, are many things in our ministry and contending for the faith: friends, comforters, lovers, fishers, workers, and *peacemakers,* and the peacemakers are blessed, along with the rest.

Be ye peacemakers, for as peace was given unto us in Christ, who now has sent the comforter on his behalf, give assurance that those who fear, suffer, and are challenged shall prevail. This peace is not for us to harbor but to sail the ocean of Man and give unto the fish of whom we are fishers.

Peace be unto you.

Do not be filled with fear, but be filled with the Holy Ghost; do not hide the ship of Christ, but sail the ocean as fishermen; do not be yoked by the Devil, but take on the yoke of Christ. If peace is yours, then it is yours to share, acting as the representatives of Christ, identified in the Word and walking through the world, not as a child who wields a sword it cannot carry, but as men and women who are trained, well-versed in the Word, having the spirit that giveth life.

Thank God for His tutors and governors.

Are you liberated by God's grace, flying high above the tumult of men, or does the death of the Law burden you? Are you afraid to do greater things than what you do, convinced by Satan's comfort that enough is simply *enough?* There is no such thing as doing "enough" for God, for he has given us talents and graces in accordance with the distribution He has sovereignly entrusted; it would be a sin to harbor such things. We must all we can for Him, and though He takes His time to mold us up in His righteousness, humbling us, sanctifying us — the saints — to His will, we should not contribute to the counterproductivity of God's production, which is producing us through Christ.

Our lives are not our own. The blood of Jesus Christ has purchased us; we are his workmanship. Though our time is limited, and so much of it has been "wasted," God redeems it. With what we've been given, we will do more than we could ever imagine, not on our own accord, but by Christ's sustaining sovereignty.

If God's word is heavy, exercise your faith muscles to carry it with the ultimate Strength Trainer: God. Recognize *Christ's* day, *Christ's* time, and *Christ's* purpose. When you do all things in him, whether suffering or pleasing, in prosperity or hardship, you will recognize that today, regardless of whether it is good or bad, blessed or cursed, backslidden or redeemed, is not only a good one but *his*, and if he is for us, who can be against us (Romans 8:31)?

Have exceeding great joy in your salvation that has been restored by the Lord, whom David gave this title via the revelation of who He was to him: The Lord of Lords and King of Kings, mighty God is He; saving us and keeping us from all sin and shame; wonderful is our redeemer, praise his name.

World of the Wicked

*W*e live in a wicked world.

This is nothing new. The world has been wicked since its fruit could be eaten, and the same fruit, paired with the other desires of the flesh, has ruled and dictated every one of Man's steps. Whether it be sexual immorality, impurity, sensuality, idolatry, sorcery, enmity, strife, jealousy, fits of anger, rivalries, dissensions, divisions, envy, drunkenness, orgies, revelry, or extortion, simplistically summarized as disobedience (Galatians 5:19-21), have all been passed down through the generations since the very beginning.

The children of this world, of darkness, are wiser than the children of God, of light, in the things of this world. They know their master better than the believers know theirs, and more than this, they have not only accepted the prince of darkness as their ruler but also taken pleasure in all his rewards. They willingly represent him in their entertainment, glorify him in the political buildings, and worship him based on his wishes so they may attain the treasures and pleasures of life:

> The master commended the dishonest manager for his shrewdness. For the sons of this world are more shrewd in dealing with their own generation than the sons of light.
> — Luke 16:8 (ESV)

But worldly things, materialistic reward with sinful application, are not a worry for the believer, for those who do not partake in evil acts, as outlined by the apostle Paul in his address to the Galatians, inherit the Kingdom of Heaven — riches beyond compare. This is mirrored in Jesus's parable of the unjust steward, who is rebuked for having two masters, unto their condemnation if they remain in their unrepentant sin. Now, we do not rejoice in the condemnation of the wicked, regardless of how horrid their actions may be, for we know the consequences of their actions and would not wish such a fate on our worst enemy, as God does not. Unfortunately, this same consequence has been portrayed as a party that the Devil has exclusively invited them to, disguising himself as a friend rather than revealing himself as the foe, who knows what wrath and judgment await him. It only seeks to kill those he hates, knowing his infinite hubris will complete his fate.

The unrighteous have been taken by the pleasures of the world, which we call the great deception, to the extent that they know the result that the wickedness of this world gets them to, and they *still* side with Satan.

His scales enthrall them as he digs his fangs into their souls, filling their every vein with venom. The deterioration of America is not only happening because we reject the Gospel but because the souls of the powerful who police our provinces have been eaten away by the cankerworm of corruption through money, fame, and fornication.

Money is fine if you don't love it, but these fellows in their forever folly prioritize it before God and make it "number one" in their lives. Christian fame is a byproduct of the man who has humbled himself and been exalted. That does not mean they are of the same fame and stature as the modern pop star, but rather that they are Christ or John the Revelator in their time. I say that though both are possible, they are not an absolute, nor evidence or expectation of the sons and daughters of God, but contingent on God's will.

That said, fornication is terrible regardless of how you slice it. Because of this, God provided the way of marriage as a means for the believer to avoid it (Hebrews 13:4). Yet we wonder why our governments have worked so hard to destroy the nuclear family, why they have perverted our modern morals, corrupted the sanctity of marriage, and normalized Epsteinian behaviors. They are simply spiking our spiritual waters with hints of the rapscallion's roofies, hoping to bring us down to a lower level so they may remain on top.

Nowadays, if you're not divorced, you're on your way. When you're on your way, you're open to all doorways to fornications. Behind one of those doors is homosexuality, and behind a smaller, child-sized door within *that* door is a far more terrible thing, a door no child, much less an adult, should enter through. Yet, here, we see the rich and powerful forcing it open and attempting to normalize it.

This world and its rulers are *wicked*. This is not stated without merit or revelation but by the word of God, which a son or daughter of Him shall declare. I am not afraid of what comes next, but I cannot say the same for the billionaires who build bunkers.

> Fret not yourself because of evildoers, and be not
> envious of the wicked, for the evil man has no future;
> the lamp of the wicked will be put out.
> — Proverbs 24:19-20 (ESV)

No bunker is fortified or deep enough to shield them from God's wrath.

They know this. They are sitting ducks, quacked out of their mind, dreading what comes next yet unwilling to accept the Solution Savior. This leads me to my final point, the inspiration of this piece: the world has made its bed and is ready and willing to sleep in it. Why have we, the children of God, not done the same with our Resting Place? We who have the promise, the revelation, the truth, and the strength, by God's grace, have not made our bed but defiled it with the world's doctrine. Unbiblical denominations, dogmas, personal vices, and lies we tell ourselves to justify our traditions and personal beliefs.

These are our greatest offenders.

Satan and his seed have reached a state where they do evil things but call it good (Isaiah 5:20). They are *cruel*. Why have we not been brought to a place where we do great things for the sake of being "good?" We should not use our gifts to be influencers who benefit ourselves, nor use Christ as a catapult to our careers to fortune and glory, but to represent the good One who is actually good: God. We should unashamedly use our gifts to edify the body of Christ, motivated by eternal life, and expecting more than materialistic rewards, but spiritual ones.

We must work; we are His.

The spiritual war that has always been fought is in full swing. The Devil is no longer in the details but in the politician, pop star, and preacher. If we are to go to war, we must turn away from the adornment of deception and instead take on the whole armor of God. Times have never been more serious. It has come to the point where insanity is the central mentality. We live in an age where, when someone asks how to come to Christ as opposed to Mohammed, you're ridiculed, criticized, and banned for "hate speech."

This is no longer a game, hobby, or Sunday morning tradition where we frolic through the flower fields of faith — it never was. It is life and death, and the servants of the Dark Master hunger not only for money, fame, and fornication but for *blood*. They desire that we all would die spiritually more than physically, for in a physical death, the believer goes to God, but in a spiritual one, the wages of sin, your soul, go to Hell in the second judgment.

This desire is their commission.

What is the great commission of the believer? To go into all the world and preach the gospel, regardless of what comes next.

Curse of the New Year

*T*here is a saying that has been touted for years, and years, and years, and years, and years, and years, and years before:

New year, new me.

It is repetitive.

Since I was a child, I've heard this New Year's saying, and thankfully, to the point of my prose, it's now seen as more of a joke, a self-aware commentary on man's inability to change his ways despite his deep-seated desire to do so, at least in modern meme culture.

"New Year? New me."

This statement is nothing more than a slogan that serves as an advertisement for the timeless, generally understood, and inescapable message: You will not change. You will repeat your actions from last year and the previous year. This is the Curse of the New Year, dooming us to an endless, repetitious walk, like the children of Israel, who walked forty years in the wilderness on their path to the Promised Land. Funnily enough, much like them, the path to paradise was straightforward. There is no grand mystery in God's simplicity; it is simply that the gate is strait and the way is narrow (Matthew 7:14). That said, on the subject of change, the only *actual* change is found in simplicity, yet is rejected and made complex in the human mind. We believe we know better than God, which is ironic and almost humorous compared to God's omniscient, omnipresent, all-powerful mind. We reject grace and replace it with the Law; confuse justification with sanctification and vindication with salvation; reject God's authority and replace it with Man's authority, whether it be a pope's, pastor's, prophet's, institution's, denomination's, or our own.

The categories are relational, but distinct, and this is where most will find condemnation rather than Christ.

If you want to change — to receive blessings rather than curses — then you must receive *Christ*. What law of man has changed a man's desires to a permanent degree? What self-help book, guru, or religion has freed a soul that addictions have bound? Can God's Law save, or is it by His grace we may obtain eternal life? Without the latter, we will never be free from the circularity of our sin, having no way to discern the malicious master of our lives who sells us to wicked slavers. If we could, we would no longer be deceived but realize we are *addicted* to sin: Drugs, alcohol, sex, money, and self-righteousness are more than an addiction to materialistic and stimulative substances, but an addiction to the dissociation, distraction, depression, and exaltation they offer. We *conceptualize* change, but *desire* the stimulant of the Wicked Wasp's stinger. We call these stimulants "good" and ourselves "holy." In this, we find irony, given that these things, even to a scientific degree, are damaging to the body and mind, and, to a spiritual degree, are condemnable. We are masochists made by putrid powers, but the Master does not subscribe to that philosophy nor those actions:

> Therefore, if anyone is in Christ, he is a new creation.
> The old has passed away; behold, the new has come.
> — 2 Corinthians 5:17 (ESV)

"New Year? New me?" No. It may be a new year, but it's the same "me" unless we choose to be in Christ, for we are a new creature *in* him. I am called a simpleton and am criticized for "oversimplifying complex issues with something as simple as God," or "being a no-good prot who is too stupid to understand the great, wondrous, amazing, historical, super-true-and-not-at-all-logical-nonsense of the one, true holy church of God" (which every cult claims). To them, I say, "Some of God's greatest revelations are found in His simplicity. Mankind complicates things, muddying Jesus's waters and obsessing over knowledge unto insanity, drastically confusing all with their many lies."

If you have faith but no works, then why should I believe you? The Christian cultist tends to love James, though they quote him out of context and determine his meanings through illiteracy. Only in a generation of blinded fools would you ever find foolish entrusting their salvation to the blind. You say you have faith? Show me your works to prove your faith; I will show you my faith by my works. I will provide evidence to my faith claim to prove that my God is true, vindicating that declaration before Man, and showing you to be a fraud. Is that simple enough for you? Straightforward? Or is it a straw man that misrepresents your nonsensical, condemnable, and wicked faith, as utterly contradictory as it is?

They say I cannot address an argument; what argument is there to address when it is based on an untruth that only survives in the circularity of logical fallacy? But oh, the brilliant minds of the organized religions have found themselves to be geniuses! Egad, they have been educated at *Flatulence University*, getting high off the air they breathe in their vacuum of vanity.

Where does my wisdom come from? God. You would know if you had known Him.

The world *needs* God, not man's laws or politicians, or institutionalized religions that take the Lord's name in vain. Though all those things have their place, *they* need Jehovah — we *all* do. To beat the curse that plagues our years, months, weeks, days, hours, minutes, and seconds, we must give Him every second, minute, hour, day, week, month, and year. We must be in Christ to become new, and when we meet these requirements, we receive the blessings written in his book. We are no longer cursed by the Master of Evil but blessed by the Master of Good. Now, we go forward on the straight and narrow, changed, breaking the habits of the generations before us, no longer stung and in pain, depressed and angry, addicted to the whips of this world, or exalted by our own egotism, but *free*, having repented, believed, and rested.

We are not made free by the standards of the world and their manmade "freedom," but by the blood of Jesus Christ, the standard that all men who strive to be better must meet before the Infinite judges them.

John Anderson

Search me, O God, and know my heart!
Try me and know my thoughts!
And see if there be any grievous way in me,
and lead me in the way everlasting!
— Psalm 139:23-24 (ESV)

The Blind Believer

*I*f my heart goes out to anyone, it is those who are lost.

Not all hearts are inspired to work in America's mission field. I know the believer is saved, but the lost are in danger of damnation. Many of my brothers, sisters, and I have felt the urge to help those who would sooner hate, slander, and prosecute us than hear what God has to say. Some might say we're fighting a losing battle, but I say what my God says: We are fighting the good fight.

We have many members in the body. Although we follow the same Scripture, the Gospel, the mission of the hand is different from the mission of the foot. Let us respect our differences and support one another on our Holy Ghost-filled journeys. It takes a brave child of God to face the American audience. Even more, it takes a believer who is filled with the Spirit of God and has the fruits of the Spirit, which are love, joy, peace, long-suffering, gentleness, goodness, and faith, to not only withstand the contrary spirits but also to exemplify Christ in our time, given that our fruits identify us.

To God's children lost in darkness, we are a light, a path to salvation, among other characteristics of the cross.

Let us define a believer. There are two types of believers in our churches and the world: the entirely lost, those in between, and those who are saved. Ultimately, these three can collapse into two: belief or unbelief; fruit or no fruit; works or no works; grace or law.

The saved, the *true* believer, is the one we are most familiar with. He loves the Father and worships in Spirit and truth. The in-between believer is the one who comes to church, fellowships with the brothers and sisters, and worships just the same, physically, but only in the life he lives on Sunday, not on any other day of which we are called to worship. He does not desire change, truly, and though he might have had an emotional experience, until he really knows Christ, it is only a matter of time before he falls away.

This believer lives two lives: One of God and the other of the world. He is lukewarm, not entirely sold out to God — he is between two masters. As we know, this cannot be so. God will eventually spew him out of his mouth. This applies to those in false doctrines as well, who might profess His name and do great works for their own vanity, but ultimately remain unknown to the God of the universe, which can then cast them into a category of unbelief. However, they believe they are within His truth.

Of the entirely lost, he is the one who does not believe in God at all, sometimes to the degree that he denies God's existence, but most times to the extent that he outright rejects Christ, usually appealing to his wants and desires, which the god of this world loves.

When we think of the phrase "the entirely lost," we assume that it means "atheist," he who denies God's existence by science. However, the lost one is more than a scientific denier; he listens to the god that propagates hundreds of thousands of false religions. Atheism (though the atheist will deny this) is a religion. You *believe* God is not real because you cannot *prove* His existence. Yes, the burden of proof is on you to prove that your evidence for a lack of God is sufficient, particularly when the apologist can prove the proof for His existence is. Therefore, you must activate your *faith* to believe what you believe, even if it is in nothing. The very denial of God's existence implies He exists, which is only furthered by the understanding that you cannot prove something *doesn't* exist and can only create an argument and hypothesis that He doesn't, which is not evidence-based but faith-based.

Show me your faith by your absence of evidence, and I will show you my faith by the evidence in your absence.

Thus, the lost are not always lost because they do not believe in God's existence, but because they have rejected God despite all the evidence showing Him, and instead believed the god of this world, who has entrapped them in his darkness, perverting their faith and placing them in their best religion.

He has made you gods, and has given you knowledge so that you may not come to have more faith in God, but so that you might worship yourself. We desire to worship; it's in our nature. Whether we worship ourselves, an institution, material idols, political parties, God, or Satan himself, we are *worshippers*.

You who advertise yourselves with your theatricality and performances: if this fits your bill, then fill the space.

There are more religious Christians who are utterly lost who believe in their religion rather than God than there are atheists or agnostics who do not think He exists. Satan is most prominent in the church, unfortunately, masquerading in counterfeit Christianity and establishing himself as the pastor of the denominations, dogmas, and cults that grow fat on false doctrine. Darkness is not always easily identified, especially when it is all you've ever known. To the blind man, darkness is simply sight. We who have seen the Light can call the darkness "darkness," but those who have not known Him cannot identify it without its contrast.

You Bartimayuses: fear not, for Jesus arrives to bring the light; if only you would hear the elected son or daughter of God who knows their place as the saved, coming to meet you for your divine appointment.

You will not find Christ in a pope nor his rebellious children, being the church of the Protestant, Eastern Orthodox, and the denominational names thereof, but in God's word that distributes His people among them, in fullness and truth, as it has been written. I am not bashing those in a denomination, but I am bringing its divisiveness to your attention. God did not ordain denominations; this is true scripturally. The hearing and accepting of the Word, making our revelation of Jesus Christ, leads to a spiritual rebirth into his body, pulling us from the world and into him, which is what the word "church" means. In Greek, ekklesia translates to "called-out assembly," as in our New Testament, new-covenant calling.

If your denomination or local church contradicts His completed Word, then you would do well to leave.

Come into God's word in its fullness; be made to see by the light. I have seen this and speak boldly on these matters, not on my own accord, but through tutors and governors. These Holy Ghost-filled men have exemplified God's ministry to me as evangelists, pastors, and teachers, who are all distributed through God's ecclesial provision. So you see, I do not disdain leadership; I abhor false leaders who send people to Hell, which is reasonable, as you might understand.

In the end, it's your decision as to whether or not you will serve the Lord, but know that once the darkness, the sin, is revealed to you, you are no longer blind but are now responsible for the sin you continue to commit. Your invincible ignorance has been depleted, and even in your ignorance, you would still be held accountable for your sin, your rejection of God, your disobedience, believing in Satan's lies rather than God's truth. Search within yourself and ask if this is true; the voice of God is heard and continues to be heard through that same voice of the letter, now more easily and continually identifiable to he who is willing to seek truth humbly. Open your eyes, Him, blind believer. See the light that is Christ. Do not be blinded by the angel of light, Lucifer, that fallen one who appeals to the populace with materialism and beauty.

Sin is beautiful; it is enticing; it looks good. To some, the word of God is "ugly," offensive, appearing harsh, brutal, and mean, especially when placed next to sin in comparison or the identity that many have established in unbiblical principles.

As is love to the one who knows love, not.

Though the way is hard, unpopular, and challenging, it is the provided way, made through that sacrifice on Calvary — the blood of Jesus Christ, who is the way, the truth, and the life.

And even if our gospel is veiled, it is veiled to those who are perishing. In their case, the god of this world has blinded the minds of the unbelievers, to keep them from seeing the light of the gospel of the glory of Christ, who is the image of God. For what we proclaim is not ourselves,

but Jesus Christ as Lord, with ourselves as your servants for Jesus' sake. For God, who said, "Let light shine out of darkness," has shone in our hearts to give the light of the knowledge of the glory of God in the face of Jesus Christ.
— 2 Corinthians 4:3-6 (ESV)

He Who Makes God Cry

*H*uman emotions are often troubling, so much so that the average believer is afraid to show them at all. Within the former, we have the archetype of the believer who has disassociated from their emotions in fear of what they might reap, insecure as to whether they have enough Holy Ghost in them to control said emotions, rather than the vehemence controlling them.

God is a God of emotions. Joy, wrath, love, and indignation exist within Him, albeit righteous, and are in us if we are where He delights to dwell. A church without emotions is arguably inhuman; this we know, and any believer afraid to feel them lives in the most prominent, contrary emotion of all: fear.

Imagine the irony.

This is not to say that we are exclusively emotional, nor should we apply human understanding to Godly concepts, for God's emotions are spiritual, just as God is a spirit (John 4:24). But we must recognize what we are comprised of if we are not only to approach matters better but also heal from the damages they have caused.

Love is more than familial or romantic; it is of God, going beyond human

intellectualism and into spirituality. Hate should not be used to justify attacks against our brothers and sisters, in and out of Christ, but rather to hate the sin, the disobedience, the deception — the Devil, who leads them to an eternally horrid end. Joyfulness is not an overcompensation for sadness, but rather a counter to the feeling, an amplifier to happiness, for both of those emotions are temporary, yet eternally exhibited in Christ.

Wrath, as terrible as it sounds, is a great motivator when fighting against Satan and his succubi, especially when the evil of this world is revealed, as it has been and will continue to be in our time. Still, giving in to wrath as your primary motivator is dangerous, for though this emotion is present, its exclusive focus on vengeance is reserved for God when the flesh is focused on.

Then there is the other archetype: the overemotional believer, the charismatic one, if you will, that modern churches and their leaders have created to replicate the Spirit of God while robbing the people of a true "Holy Ghost experience." They do not follow the model God has established, but rather their business model that creates repeat customers. The devil can pervert and impersonate the Spirit of God. Still, there is only one God, one Spirit, one mind, one word, one son, one Father, and one Son, and His characteristics and outcomes are not only clearly written in the Bible, but also coequal and coeternal.

Whatever is done that does not agree with this is not of God and should be identified as such, for your sake.

You who rest your salvation (which is every one of us): What do you rest your salvation in? Christ or a church? The denominations have established a way, but it is not the way, in most cases, not because the decently and orderly church can't be established, but because human beings can err. In the American-made church, this is their way — these wolves in sheep's clothing that lead you to damnation in place of doctrine so they may line their pocketbooks on earth rather than multiply their riches in Heaven. The church has become a club, a place to dance to secular music with the label "Christian" slapped to the surface, meaning that they worship themselves and not Christ — exalt ourselves and not Him; make ourselves the heroes when we are nothing but a doer of good that we cannot derive from ourselves. It is complete with a light show and emotion-based preaching that perfectly complements choreographed experiences similar to those of Hollywood. The word of God is not a show; it is not a put-on, emotion-exclusive experience that allows you to go clubbing "safely," away from sex, booze, and drugs.

He is intimate, sincere, and feels where he is believed: in the heart. Unfortunately, that does not make the Catholic sacramental mass any better, nor does the Eastern Orthodox practice differ. It is a different side of the same coin, equally as emotional but practiced slightly differently.

Except, ironically, in those theologies, that worship comes with dogmas that will send you to Hell (more on that another day).

So, we must ask ourselves, "Where is the balance?"

I believe the Bible makes it quite clear: "Jesus wept" (John 11:35, ESV). However, if we keep reading, we'll notice an interesting dichotomy: "Lazarus, come out" (John 11:43, ESV).

What was the purpose of his groaning, then? Why is God grieved? Why did the God-man shed tears? After all, was this not the very same Jesus who opened the eyes of the blind man?

Emotions are a natural human element; they are also God's. God, as He looks upon us, can be grieved (Genesis 6:6). The Holy Spirit, being God among us, is grieved the same by our actions (Ephesians 4:30). In this case, Christ felt and faced these elements for a different reason: out of sheer empathy and compassion for the misery of His creation. He was moved by such a sad moment, this groaning and moaning that His creation feels.

Imagine how much more He feels on an infinitely global scale? If He wept over the city of Jerusalem, the murderers of the prophets (Luke 19:41; 13:34), those He knew would not be saved because of their unrepentant unrighteousness. Still, though he felt them, they were overcome by His own power to work the miracle of Lazarus and complete the mission of Jerusalem, so that it would display the works of God to whosoever would around Him.

In a human sense, emotions are a motivator, a fuel, that ties us to a fight via personal stakes. They are not to be ignored but felt and used only when applied with the Holy Ghost, God, within us, which is to say to be discerned biblically. When we are happy, God is glad; when we are sad, God empathizes with the sadness; when we laugh, God laughs; when we cry, God wipes away the tears; when God is angry at the Devil, we are furious at him also, but in all these things we must let no emotion lead us to sin, overcoming everything and doing what it is we have been sent here to do by Him, as Jesus exemplified.

Who is he who makes God cry? Those dead who are the same as Lazarus, the unrepentant, as Jerusalem. Why? We who are mortal should see the tragedy of the world and its state and be *grieved*, groaning for a better outcome, and sorrowful, not because it is all hopeless, but because the Spirit of God in us cries out, knowing the coming consequence for those who reject Christ entirely by their sense of self. God desires all to be saved; so do we: Friends, family, and all who are being deceived, the lost souls who are being led astray, for we know the wages of sin. Let us not sit in the emotion alone, nor ignore the human element that God has placed within us, but take on the Holy Ghost to have those spirit-fueled emotions, to tell the Lazaruses of this world to *come forth*.

The Doctrine of Doom

*T*he church is in great peril.

I, who walk the Earth as my brothers and sisters do, have seen the same works and beliefs of the doctrinally devoid denominations and have come to a different conclusion than the family I walk with, especially concerning eternal life. Confusion and false doctrine have gripped the church and its people, perverting God's word in its perfect form (as given) and projecting a doctrine of doom that leads the people to damnation. The false prophets that Christ warned us about have founded churches, set up shop on a non-scriptural, manmade concept that God never ordained. This is no surprise, however, given that the doctrine of the Devil is far more appealing than the Word of God. Man and its church leaders have chosen to align with hate, esoteric knowledge, and "new revelation" of the fallen angel rather than the angel of the Lord. They choose the popular faith, the surface-level belief that does not produce life but rather zeroes behind a primary value in their bank accounts, rather than the unchanging and completed Word:

> Jesus Christ is the same yesterday and today and forever.
> — Hebrews 13:8 (ESV)

In the rule of the profiteer, we find a mathematical truth wherein anything multiplied by zero is still zero. Where there is God, there is life, whereas wherever Satan goes, death follows: The wages of sin are death, yet he who believes in Christ shall have (currently) eternal life. We are not condemned in Christ. You cannot ignore this (Romans 8:1). In multiple examples, primarily on social media platforms, we see believers who say they believe in Christ yet do not do what He says we should do. Influencers profess the Word of God, which is honorable, scriptural, and good, but they do not present themselves as the spirit of God would command them to: in modesty. Thus, though they say, "Lord, Lord," they are not known and are only tools in the hands of the devil, sent to doom more people than ever before.

We sell out for materialism and propagate such ideals with compromises on our faith, holding hands with false doctrines in the name of "unity" when the better term is "uniformity" unto conformity to condemnable heresies. We are Crawfordian in nature, appealing to the vast Catholic audience conveniently after creating a Holy-Spirit-inspired energy drink to make millions in the name of God.

For clarity, I have no issue getting paid for sharing the Gospel; I take issue with compromising on your faith to do so, for in that case, you are not spreading the Gospel, but sending people to Hell for the sake of a good paycheck. Those who do this partake in the doctrine of doom, platforming the Shamoun-type who disguise their hatred as "the love of God," when we should be rebuking them before all, so that others may stand in fear. It is this type of unwise behavior that deceives many, who lack the self-control and wisdom to discern the unfruitful. Allegorically, I compare this to modesty standards: yes, we should not dress in a manner that sexualizes ourselves to others, making us far more physically appealing, but it is also up to the individual to have enough of the Holy Ghost in them to withstand the temptation they are exposed to. We are not exempt from consequences simply because we are ignorant, deceived, or led astray by false teachers.

We are held accountable by our decisions; the sin is still actual, and when we lend ourselves to a spirit that does not value the soul that Christ has purchased, we invite lust in. Spiritual leaders will be held responsible for your fellowship with the fiend that has caused another who either looks at them or looks up to them to fall, the same way we will be held accountable for looking at the appeals of men and entreating. I encourage you to check your subconscious, motive, and objective, for we are warned that those who are enticed (when coming to know Christ), if they do not know Him as more than enlightenment, the taste of the heavenly gift, the sharing of the Holy Spirit, the goodness of the Word of God, the powers of the age to come, will fall away. For they did not know the surety of the better things — the things that belong to salvation. (Hebrews 6:4, 9). We are not of those who shrink back and are destroyed, but of those who have faith and preserve their souls (Hebrews 10:39), understanding that He keeps us. Therefore, those who profess Christianity but are not possessed by Christ were not of us, for if they were, they would have continued (1 John 2:19).

I understand this is a harsh rebuke, but I say it with love. This is comparable to those who dance to demonic-secular music (propagating bad messages) and wear tight clothes or no clothes at all for attention. Understand that I am not criticizing your natural features, which you cannot change, but rather the mentality and spirit behind them, which you can. In a natural sense, I am no stranger to this psychology. I know that my features would be described as "fair to look upon," and have been described that way on many occasions, being compared to a beastly figure because of my tall stature, curly hair, and way with words, which is ironically an antisemitic sentiment that originates from Serpent Seed, not any descriptor in the Bible.

Though I will admit… I do look Jewish. Perhaps I am? Because of this, I have faced much antisemitism, particularly from catholics. I'm not making a point here; I just wanted to add it because it's my lived experience and something I needed to share.

This is no fault of mine but the handiwork of God, which is both out of my control and yours. That said, we can control our intentions, which are often misleading. Many of us would prefer people look at us rather than Christ, yet we use his name to garner an audience. We use God as a niche for influence, the same way the world uses its allurements. But if the fisherman who uses the lure does not have life within him, he will only be a fisherman who collects fish for killing, but does not cast, and eats without knowing starvation.

To that end, you might as well partake in the world's offerings, for by your fruits, you are known, and one cannot have two masters. Why not partake in the fruit of Genesis and serve the master of the world? Why not grow your knowledge through disobedience rather than through faith in God?

This is the world's religion, the doctrine of doom.

It is similar to women in pastoral positions: unbiblical, yet accepted, and when you rebuke such a false doctrine, you are met with gnashing of teeth and wailings of hatred. Do not let the spirits provoke you to sinful anger, for it is not the Word we should be insecure about, but gracious in its conviction.

I must remind you that these words are not my own; this truth is the Word of God, in accordance with Paul, who clearly outlined what an elder is and, by deductive reasoning, what he isn't:

> Therefore an overseer must be above reproach, the husband of one wife, sober-minded, self-controlled, respectable, hospitable, able to teach, not a drunkard, not violent but gentle, not quarrelsome, not a lover of money. He must manage his own household well, with all dignity keeping his children submissive, for if someone does not know how to manage his own household, how will he care for God's church? He must not be a recent convert, or he may become puffed up with conceit and fall into the condemnation of the devil. Moreover, he must be well thought of by outsiders, so that he may not fall into disgrace, into a snare of the devil.
> — 1 Timothy 3:2-7 (ESV)

To the few who claim, "Nay," they have inspired this piece, saying, "Not only is Paul not alive to write an address to the church, but the address he did write was for the Corinthians in a different time," I write to you, saying, "It was not Paul who penned the parliament, but the Holy Spirit. The same One that was in Paul is the same spirit that is co-equal and co-eternal with the Son and the Father, and thus, (given God is His word) the Bible is eternal — timeless."

What was relevant then is relevant now. What was alive then is alive today. To this end, if you believe the contrary, which is that what Paul wrote is not eternal, then you say that the Holy Ghost is not infinite, which is to say that Christ is not immortal, which is to say that Christ is not the Word made flesh.

This is a doctrine of the antichrist that would doom us all, if possible.

The misrepresentation of God's word can't be simplified by calling it an opinion, for it is far more dangerous than this and insulting to the Spirit of God. Therefore, if you need a present-Paul, let the Spirit of God be Paul to you, alive today, not only in His people but especially in the living Word. The same Spirit is in those who seek the truth, even taking this address as more than an opinionated or "misogynistic" piece, but as the truth that can be seen in the Word of

God. If you don't like what I'm writing, then please go to the scriptures above that God already wrote. Still, I would not blame you if you didn't see it that way, for that same antichrist spirit that was present, crucifying Christ, murdering the martyrs, and possessing the Pharisees, is alive and well today. The antichrist will come in embodiment, but his message is here now, growing alongside the wheat as a weed, being watered by the same waters.

We should all desire to follow the will of God, walking in obedience and setting aside our desires. If you cannot handle sitting down rather than going up behind a pulpit or pastoring a flock, then that is nothing more than ego talking. As a matter of fact, every other ministry, including being a mother to your children, a wife to your husband, an evangelist online or in person, among so many others. There is much good teaching and valuation in these things, not seen as lesser but equally important to the man's role. He has his responsibilities as you do yours, and is the authority in the household that you should not usurp authority over, but respect as he has respected you. If he has not done these things, it is not an excuse nor justification to act outside of God's word, but an opportunity to cling closer to it, unto the manifestation of Christ's testimony, and rebuke when biblically necessary, understanding and weighing all things with wisdom.

God has finished His Word. He does not ask us to interpret it through our modernized views, but to believe in Him, taking Him at His word and hearing Him for what He says, knowing how to read in context. The husband is the head of the wife, in the same way that Christ is the head of the church. This is the way of the Lord, the truth in this world, the life of a believer: to submit to Christ, above all else, regardless of gender or our influence. There are so many biblical ways we can glorify God in the Bible.

Through the gifts, we edify the body. As spouses, we can support our partners. In parenthood, the greatest of these, will there be glorification of God when we raise our children in the way of the Lord so they will not depart from Him? The role of the mother and father is so important, nay, essential, and the modern Christian so *tirelessly* fights against it because of the societal norms set by those who do not value them. It is a beautiful ministry. It's not for everybody, but it's wonderful, nonetheless.

We all have a simple calling with obvious attributes and characteristics for leadership and submission to leadership. The calling is to go into the world and preach the Gospel in the ways they are instructed to under Holy-Ghost-filled tutors and governors, with power, love, and a sound mind, through Spirit and truth and by the Word of God. With this, we add the fruits of the Spirit, the characteristics of the Holy Ghost-filled individual. As simple as they seem, they raise the question: If they are so simple, why do so many not have them? Particularly men, in my view, I have seen a great apostasy of godly leaders who claim to know God but are everything other than what a godly man would be. Modern men are cowards: Abusive, angry, weak, faithless (1 Timothy 5:8).

The coward is a coward because he does not say what he must, which is the God-taught truth. Regardless of whom we speak to, their position, or our place within the church, online or not, we must speak the truth of God because it is the only word worth saying. Because of our cowardice or lust for power, we have caused others to stumble and to sin — some even to reject Christ. Some even try to course correct, but they do so by unbiblical means, making slanderous condemnations against us just (Romans 3:5-8). We set a terrible example for the entirely lost, and are all held accountable for such sinful deeds. I am not alien to them; I can admit that; you should, too. Two wrongs do not make a right; the right is God's word. So, believers, stand up and on God's Word in every respect, treating your wives as Christ treats the church, as a Holy-Spirit-sealed believer would, preaching the Gospel for all to hear in all aspects of your lives, living it even in the smallest accounts.

Just because you are the head of your home does not mean you can bite off the heads of the ones beneath you; just because you are a leader over a large flock does not mean you can discount your stewardship. No amount of emotional, mental, spiritual, or physical abuse is acceptable, and any form of negligence, lack of precedence for wisdom, or biblical discernment is either. Be slow to anger, quick to be patient, merciful, and quick to Scripture, understanding the weaker vessels and your position as a leader over what God has given you.

You are responsible not only for your life but also for others'. You should know that.

Be strong. Stand upright and believe in God and His word from beginning to end, knowing the Father holds us in our perfect position in the church of Christ — those who are called out. By these means, we will not be confused by the doctrine of doom, but knowing the truth in all capacities, until the Lord comes.

Spirit of the Grieved

*G*rieving is something we all do. It is not exclusive to a particular archetype, character, individual, or circumstance but rather inclusive, involving all and being felt by everyone, primarily and most incomprehensibly by God. There are many scriptures about grieving the spirit, and almost all of them, if not all, are set in the context of the God of hope, the God of love, our God, the Lord Almighty. I find this unfathomable because God, who is exalted above all, can be distressed and sad. I suppose this is not surprising when those who cause such grief are us, who, through our actions, can cause utter sadness for the one who holds us, continually.

We cause much heaviness and sorrow; plainly speaking, we make God feel *sorry* for us. Despite my inability to intellectually grasp God's grief, I find it easy to take hold of it spiritually, for I have felt the same, and now I feel it especially. The Holy Ghost writes through our beloved brother, the apostle Paul, "For I do not do the good I want, but the evil I do not want is what I keep on doing. Now if I do what I do not want, it is no longer I who do it, but sin that dwells within me" (Romans 7:19-20, ESV). This is the fragility of humanity in our fallen state: We make mistakes, do what our flesh wants, and let God down *constantly*.

Thank God no such sin could separate us from His love… right?

"And do not grieve the Holy Spirit of God, by whom you were sealed for the day of redemption."
— Ephesians 4:30 (ESV)

    Our sins have bled Christ dry; our arrogance has frustrated, even hindered, the Spirit; our lack of discipline distresses Him. When thinking about this, I am reminded of myself as a child who, after doing something I shouldn't have done, having known better but choosing to do it anyway, was not always told by my parents how angry they were, but rather, to a more cutting end, how *disappointed* they were.

This was and is a terrible feeling, and yet, as awful as it was to have my Mom and Dad mad at me, it was far *worse* to have them disappointed, saddened, distressed, and *grieved*. It was as though the punishment inflicted on me was enough, if not *more* than enough, to get the message across, encouraging change.

God is like this with us, disappointed in our lack of discipline and abundance of arrogance that encourages us to make mistakes rather than overcome them. I am guilty of this, just as any; I thank God that He is one of mercy and forgiveness. He takes away the guilty charge we bear in our self-inflicted punishment, produced by our missteps and backslidings. The same grievance that moved God upon the children of Israel, who knew God and His ways and still sinned, finding themselves in times of great sorrow, is present today, ready to make a change for the betterment and perfect progression.

Again, I find myself thinking about the word "children." The *Children* of Israel: remembering myself as a child, and when I was a *child,* I did childish things, but as a man, I put them away (1 Corinthians 13:11). We are no longer children, physically. Time has ensured this, running through us, aging our mortal coil, and taking us to an expected, unavoidable, ever-nearing end. We are grown men and women, His children by name and identification, known as sons and daughters of God, sent to do a work that can only be done in our limited time and mortality, but instead of *doing* what we have been sent to do, we do that which we were *not*. Instead of using our gifts for the edification of the body of Christ, we hoard them selfishly and let them rot, collecting dust as we mold from the inside out, turning rotten and eventually to dust as we are told we will go.

We sadden God when we do those things, acting as ungodly thieves who grow gluttonous on God's food — His word and revelation — harboring it for ourselves in surplus. Our gifts are for the people, and if we are as we claim, which is a collective that is the body, then we must come together to do God's will. In Christ, we are more than conquerors — killers of the enemy, who are the principalities that plague us. However, if we give in to sin, then we will not live nor produce life, but die and be grieved.

If we can die to ourselves, we are born again, walking in perfection; if we live in habitual sin or accept the law as our justification, we are dead already.

My grievance is my inability to set aside my emotions and thoughts, so that my brothers' backslidings do not cause me to backslide. Instead, I should pray for my brother or sister, applying the same mercy and love that God showed me when I did the same to Him. If I am to judge, then by that same standard, I am judged and weighed in the balance and found wanting, for I want that which God does not desire to give rather than choose that which God has given. Instead of using my gifts, I set them aside, listening to the Devil's deceptions, focusing on a gift that, though God-given and soon to bear fruit, will come to fruition in *His* time.

I pray I will not sit, letting the ripened fruits rot while I wait for the unripe. I encourage you, my friends, to no longer act as children but as men and women of God, even servants and warriors in the midst of and overcomers of the adversary. Let us be filled with the Spirit of God who handles the grief. Having dealt with it, He is present to carry us through our own.

Let us do as He has done for us, for all our brothers and sisters, even going so far as to say that we would do it for our sakes.

I See the Storm

I see the storm on the horizon; I am not the only one. These times, this election year, feel off and silent. The rumors of wars are spoken of daily, and the threats to both nations (being America and the nation of God) heighten *rapidly*. With every passing day, nearly every passing hour, something new is presented, bearing its teeth and looking for the nearest neck to sink them in. Civil war is discussed as commonplace, the same way World War III is discussed, as though it's a typical conversation over coffee. This offended part of me, while the other part understands.

I understand this is the fulfillment of the scriptures, but I am offended by the ten kings' affronts to the people; I see the storm coming.

    the clouds are like mountains, without rigidity in form
    instead, they move freely and expand like an ominous idea
    i wonder how many see this same darkness and
    are thankful for the not-so-gentle giant
    taking on this formation rather than that of
    a mushroom

What time are we in where the choices we have been provided by the money-grubbing galavants are to be flooded or reduced to ash? Even now, I care not to continue the conversation pushed by the world's overlords from their high places attained through the permissive powers of principalities. I only mention this discussion so we may analyze the storm coming and encourage the believer by saying, *"Do not fear."* Much to the disciples' relatability, when faced with a storm worthy of flipping a boat in a small body of water between two lands — the Sea of Galilee — the men came to Christ in fear, worried they would soon be tipped over. When he awoke, seemingly annoyed, he commented on their little faith before rising and taking control of the storm with only three words:

"Peace, be still."

The men marveled (Mark 4:35-41).

This is what Jesus, who is the Word, who is God, made flesh, says… but what do you say? Do you believe the storm of the disciples could be the same storm of today? Do you believe that Christ can stop the storm so that you may marvel? After all, what manner of man is this that even the winds and the sea obey him? Is it only the Christ of the crucifixion, of days passed, kept upon the cross to be worshipped in death, or is he the Christ of the same yesterday, today, and forever, who is risen?

Many have Christ on the cross but not glorified in Heaven, interceding as our perfect High Priest forever (Hebrews 4:14-16; 7:25). They believe that the storms are only found in stories, that these past tempests are the only ones Christ can concur with, not the typhoons of today, assuming that Christ does not have complete control, bringing us to our completion which is the doctrine of false denominations. This is because the devil has convinced the Christian that Christ is not able to hold the believer in his hand, for the "believer" has convinced himself that he can jump out. Despite the storm being alive and well — *booming* if you will, fear-mongering the masses, thrashing all types of people about, they do not run to Christ in fear, but themselves. "Which Christ?" I ask. Now, there are a hundred-fold more false Christs than the true one, and they seek not to calm the storm but to throw their followers *into it.*

What manner of man is *this,* that he would love the winds and is subject to the powers of the sea, feeding the lost souls to it to retain his false faculty! In the perversion of this scripture, you can see the sleight of hand, the *significant* difference it makes.

I see the storm. I do not fear it, not because I am some great man, for I am the least among you, but because of the One I am within and is within me. I am no better than any of you, my brothers and sisters; I have been held amid the cyclone of the sacrilegious and am more grateful by the day. The spiritual maelstrom grows like cancer, leeching off the life of the believer without their consent, without care, perverting their life at the cellular level, and bringing nothing but *death*. Worse than this, he does it with ease, for the believer does not fight because they know not how, or worse, they refuse to, fighting for the devil rather than the Lord. They have been taken by the beauty of the blizzard in its blossoming, for storms, if viewed from a comfortable place such as a home with a fire of peace and rest, can be seen as sightly. In contrast, the homeless man, the one within the storm, realizing the truth of nature's forces, sees the reality: no man is safe lest he has the power to control the cloudburst. Alas, all storms are beautiful until lightning strikes you, washes you away, or worse, drowns you by the oceans of Man because your ship, your unbiblical theology, is taken by the sea.

This is to say that there is such a thing as peace and rest in the storm; there is also a deceptive rest that lures you into a false sense of security. They are close, nearly interchangeable analogies, which is how deceptive the Devil tends to be. Therefore, we must ask again, paraphrasing: Do you believe in Christ? Do you see the storm? Like Peter, do you stand atop the waters, or will the water take you? By faith, I answer, saying, "As long as you keep your eyes on Christ, even if you fall, you will walk again, for he will reach in and pull you from the seafarers."

We are his; anyone in his hand cannot be taken from him (John 10:28).

We are representatives, images, and if you identify yourself in Him and He in you, the winds and sea will not rock your boat unto destruction. His power will be obtained. *Then* the people of this world would say, "What manner of man is this, that even the winds and the sea obey him!" This is the scriptural vindication, proving you by His word — the endurance through tribulation and trial that glorifies God. We are His workmanship — the written epistles read of all men, the evidence of God, sent to those who will believe, which may currently be entirely lost.

Do not be afraid of the storm; be its *challenger*. These ten kings (nothing compared to the Lord) shall fulfill their destiny, but not without offense, without the children of God going into the world fearless of the storm, testifying to the Master of it to the lost ones. I challenge the principles of the popular party. I will face the storm, not alone, but with you, my brothers and sisters, beside me, for we are not at our best by ourselves, but rather together, in Christ, with him in us. Yes, I see the storm, but now, as a light of this world, standing firm for the

Lighthouse, I ask, "Storm, do you see Christ?" I pray that you do and will take his hand, regardless of all you have done.

Those who identify with Satan will be of his kin, and those who identify with Christ will be his. Those who wish to be the children of darkness will only seek to destroy the light, whereas the children of light will shine in their darkness, knowingly and unknowingly, removing it. It is a *shame* that some would choose to kill us (and may succeed) by the ordinance of God's will. Even so, in choosing to do so, they will know it was done by God's grace, granting them another chance to see Christ in his sacrifice, though they were consenting unto our death. Although Christ sits on his throne of grace, he will stand, not to bring the destruction of the redeemed, but judgment of the unbeliever.

It is damnation or redemption.

The redeemed, the Bride of Christ, is destroyed and reconstructed here on earth, receiving her covering from judgment and being made new by the obtained mercy of God's gracious throne. In contrast, the disbeliever shall be judged on that great and terrible day of the final judgment, the Second Death.

Who might he be to you on that day? The Bridegroom or the Judge? The return of Christ is great to the believer, but to the disbeliever, it is terrible. Your end shall be brought through your beauty, your storm, your *weapon* of mass destruction that blossoms and blooms, drawing nearer like a coming cloud, the mushroom bomb that harnesses the power of the atom.

The fungus grows; the cancer spreads; the storm comes, but behold, the Son of Man will be riding on the cloud that is greater than all Oppenheimer could have created.

An Address to the Pope

Given the nature of this address and those to whom it is addressed, I find it best to clarify the spirit, intention, and ordainment behind this text: I come to declare the name of the Lord Jesus Christ — to spread the Gospel, the truth, ordained by the power of God, who is within us.

I write to you in a spirit of love, which is God, understanding that God is a spirit and love, and what you have aligned yourself with, and whom you serve, at least by your claim. In doing so, the intention is not so much to write to you. Still, your followers (those whom you lead like lambs to the slaughter in the name of the Father, the Son, and the Holy Ghost), but to let my boldness of such an address grab their attention, at the least, for devout Roman Catholics may not entertain such thoughts of the Gospel if it were not for the controversy of their souls.

This is, after all, a game of souls.

I, addressing you as a pawn sacrifice, make way for the King who checks the mate you have chosen to defile your bed with. I pray you understand the harshness of my phrasing, understanding that it is scriptural, which is the foundation of this address. I have found that we often get caught up in taking past each other rather than actually addressing the central issues of the points that your church has presented in muddying manners. Some conversations on these things can be rather illuminating, while others can even impart eternal life. At the very least, I would hope that both sides would aim to represent Jesus Christ. Unfortunately, most of us are more concerned with creating a defense for God by ill-mannered means than with presenting a fair case that contends for biblical truth — the faith — rather than proving that we are the greatest keyboard cowboys in the Wild West of the internet.

Our doctrine has become denominational and dogmatic, and justification for them has been conjured out of hypersensitivity. We all have the spiritual intuition to *know* the truth when we have it; even if the demons can identify Christ by looking at him, surely we can recognize him by hearing. So, to what point is the emotional aspect of the conversation beneficial?

Then again, though faith comes by hearing, rhetorical polemic has never been unbiblical, as long as it is properly applied.

In all honesty, I would say that (as for myself), I do quite well with your fruitless flock. It usually takes a solid week of being called every name under the sun, hated on, insulted, and even racially attacked before I get to my tipping point and finally punch back, to which you're following promptly, crying about the moment it happens. I would expect nothing less from indoctrinated automatons, but that does not negate the emotional grievances your people have given me in their fighting, bickering, gnashing, and wailing when they hear the truth of the Gospel.

That's partially your fault, mind you. You propagate this.

The demons oppressing their chosen vessels cause this reaction, in my opinion. Then again, there are simply some people who are just offended by the Gospel. I say this not in demonization but in reminding us of our common enemy and in understanding that the individual fuels, enables, and empowers the principalities through their fear or hubris. I see it as an anointing nonetheless, or at the least that they are a servant for Satan, and I have biblical precedent and personal experience to back up my claim. Your people, my people, become defensive when contending for the truth, for Christ. I understand this and counsel them to the best of my ability. Still, at a certain point, like Paul, I shake my garments, recognizing that their blasphemous and unreasonable blood is on their heads.

I am not interested in arguing with fools; I am in the business of saving souls. Thus, I write boldly for their sake.

The inspiration for this text was given after having a conversation with one of your own who, after starting a fight, could not provide scriptures to support his claims and, in their place, provided man-made doctrine supplied by your institution, contradicting Christ to a great degree. Therefore, upon playing this game fairly, *I* offered a defense for him, given that he could not, which was that we must have a source on the grounds of God's word. This source can be considered questionable to a degree, but it will always be the ultimate truth. Yes, *we* can question the verifiability of the men who compiled the text and ask questions about the scriptures we do not understand. Still, the option for us to question God's word does not mean that we should, nor should we ever do it to the extent that we question God, which, as you know, is Luciferian. Such questions can lead to contradictions and theologians who consider themselves more knowledgeable than God.

I am discussing the Bible, the only foundation of our faith, in all its timelessness.

Ironically, theologians, historians, and general intellectuals question this text, compiled and written by the Jewish oracles of the Old Testament and the Messianic Jews of the New, all completed by God and recognized by the early church, which was certainly not Roman Catholic. I understand why they do not like this fact. What I *don't* understand is how someone could be so blatantly asinine, despite the Bible confirming such origins of Scripture (Romans 3:2; Luke 24:44), and a cursory reading of history does as well. From Moses to the prophets to the apostles, we have our Scripture. Jesus said so, yet catholics seem to believe that in recognition of the scriptures, they somehow wrote it and have authority over it.

They must have been a real treat on the elementary school playground, claiming the swing that already existed and saying, "It's mine," though they have no ownership.

Alas, it does not persuade me. Still, by following the argument of these individuals and their line of questioning God's word, we must apply that same criticism to *your* doctrine, texts, Bible, and beliefs, which your representative declined to do. Suppose we are to be critical of the compilation of the Bible, God's word sent to us. Though this man (in my opinion) held quite an unorthodox justification for why Sola Scriptura is unbiblical, I will address his claim, which is refuted by asking, "If a man writing a book makes it impossible for us to interpret properly, then all other texts written by men now fall into that same category. If the Bible is no good, neither are any scientific journals, religious texts by the Church Fathers, or denominational manuscripts for edifying.

By those standards, it is *all* a farce. If this is true, then what hope do we have?

The better question is more centralized on the validity of Scripture in its authoritative position as the Word of God, producing our faith, and therefore bringing us to one of two conclusions:

1. We need the church to interpret the Bible.
2. We need the Bible to interpret the Church.

If the Bible is to be interpreted by the Roman Catholic Church, then the Church is the ultimate authority, not God. If we must trust in your ex cathedra (hyperbolically speaking) to understand what the Bible means, then the text is now declared insufficient because, though you claim your magisterium does not domineer over it, it is your magisterium that has the final say, not the text. After all, you have already interpreted the portions you like, and do not want your following reading any others until the point of coming to their own conclusion, especially if it might disagree with the "church."

At that point, why even read the Bible?

However, if we need the Bible to interpret the Church, then God retains authority and can guide us through all manners of learning (John 14:26) so that we may know what is from Him and what is not. This only makes sense to me, as men can err, and though you claim God is working through the Roman Catholic Church (exclusively), I take great issue with that, knowing that we cannot make your theologies align with the text you built your church upon.

Did your church fall out of the sky? Of course not!

You built it upon God's Word that was in vast circulation at the time of its recognition. It would have survived with or without "you" because God is in control. That is our hope, and I retain that our hope is in Christ Jesus, the God of hope, who has given us the Holy Ghost, making us all unified by that One Word. This is to say that we are now at the showdown, where we must check who we are married to and have engaged with. We must identify who our husband-man is and whom we call master, and we can only do that by Scripture.

The believer has faith, and through faith, we know God. Therefore, understanding that God is visualized spiritually and intellectually, we *believe* that the Bible was written and compiled under the inspiration of the Holy Spirit. In *this*, we find hope; we see the truth exclusively. Anything added to or taken away from it results in curses and damnation. Anything contradictory to it will have the same result. The word of God is a perfect text, and any individual's disbelief in this is not a testament to its fallacy but an exemplification of what a lack of revelation unto confession can do to a soul.

You have contributed to this confusion, which is the Devil's attributes rather than God's.

Praying to dead saints for eternal life is a deception, though you claim they are alive, though dead. Alive in Christ? Sure! Able to be contacted? No. The placement of Mary as an intercessor worthy to be praised is a fallacy. Your papal placement as the mouthpiece of God is a position held arguably by the antichrist, at least in similarity, but particularly if you have convinced over a billion to follow you. It is paganism in its newest form, taken over by the persecutors before you.

I understand this cuts to the heart and is hard to read. I also understand that this is not a complete argument for my case on Catholicism, and that is intentional. I mostly aim to get your people's attention and drive at the heart of the issue, which is that the truth must be proven by our original Gospel that was and is provided by God, who is Christ and the Holy Ghost, not the Gospel must be proven by the Church.

The latter is only true if you submit to Rome; the former is true if you submit to one God, one word, one kingdom, one truth, one way, and one life.

This leads me to my final point: the revelation of Jesus Christ. How does one attain the revelation of who Christ is to us, unto the confusion of their faith, the repentance thereof, and the complete change of nature? Is it through Man and his institutions? Through you? The priests? The sacraments?

As far as Hebrews is concerned, those have been done away with, and now we have the Comforter. How do I know this? I am a simple writer who pens this to you as a living sacrifice, meant to be martyred and forgotten in favor of the souls we play for. In short, the bastardization of the Gospel throughout history reveals the Roman Catholic Church's contributions to vulgar deeds committed in the vain name of the Lord. Arguments could be made that you match the description of the one in Revelation 17:5. Alas, you were the first church and the first to fall. From there, the denominations sprouted, and everyone has leavened the bread, here a little, there a little, favoring manmade dogma over biblical doctrine and self-proclaimed divinity over deferentialism.

I encourage you to examine these things on your own. Understand that this is not written to put down my brothers and sisters in the denominations but to encourage them to rise higher and, more importantly, out of the church of the world. Question whether or not the Holy Spirit seals you, that your salvation is sure, and that you can rest your eternal life on faith in Christ Jesus. Do not hesitate to *run* to Christ if you have any doubt or feel anything wrong in your heart.

Do not worship a man, office, religion, denomination, dogma, theologian, apostolic genealogy, or prophet, but Jesus Christ. This Word was made flesh and is the very same God that is in us today. Those who believe God's word to the last letter, as it is written, believing in Him with the faith of a mustard seed, know that he is our hope, love, life, and truth, among an infinite number of other titles and promises that He has rightfully earned.

> For there is one God, and there is one mediator between God and men, the man Christ Jesus, who gave himself as a ransom for all, which is the testimony given at the proper time.
> — 1 Timothy 2:5-6 (ESV)

I hope you will attain the promise of Abraham.

A sharp rebuke,

John Anderson

The Importance of the Church

I pray this letter finds you in the same hope of wellness that I have for you, having confidence that you will take it in its intended spirit. I write to you with love; this is made possible by the Holy Spirit that Christ has given us. In saying this, I greet you in his name, the name above all names, the Word made flesh, who is alive and well, living among us, within us.

I am an observer, among many things. In my observations, I often see the many illusory ways that the Devil works within the wind. His army, Legion, comes in like a flood, washing away all who do not stand upon the solid rock-revelation of Christ. This happens in different ways, time and time again, with various subjects. Unfortunately, once an individual catches wind of a contrary thought and does not recognize it as contrary, they use social media to evangelize in our modern day. He spreads a false doctrine like wildfire with its powers, parroting it before without checking it with the mind of Christ. I draw attention to this observation for this reason: The enemy has many titles, and an observer is among them. He has observed, nay, even known us far longer than we have known ourselves. Like me, he watches and waits.

In fairness, not many know their scriptures well enough to understand that false prophets speak to them, mainly because the world's pastors lack the courage, discipline, and desire to preach doctrine. They value popularity over people and likability over love. Hence, the reason I am so critical of the denominations is not that I hate the people within them, or even the slight doctrinal differences we have, nor the organizational aspect of it, but because I love them. Like my Father, I do not desire that all of you be fooled, taken by the devil's tricks. This is the same conclusion concerning denominations that you all have come to on your own, by the leading of our Lord Jesus Christ: They are fine until they become divisive, deceptive, damaging, deadly, or dangerous. It is those identifiers that warn us of Satan, and even with proper revelation, he can deceive a believer.

As we have established, the church, according to Scripture, is not a building but a people. Remember the term ekklesia, a "called-out assembly." This states that God calls you out of the world to be in His body. Some confuse this with going to a physical church or holding beliefs different from the world's, to a moral and spiritual degree, while others claim that they believe in God while still being part of the world. There is only one way to the Father, to Heaven, and that is through Christ, not our church, denomination, or creed, but through him. With this revelation, we understand the meaning of being born again in the Spirit, for in being born again, we realize that the body of Christ, the church, is a nation of individuals with the same spirit: the Holy Spirit, radically changed and eternally preserved.

Thus, the exodus of believers leaving churches and denominations is, to some degree, revelatory and expected by others. A proper exodus is performed in understanding that going to church does not save us, but saved people will go to church; fellowship does not save us, but fellowshipping is something a believer does; a single church is not our only fellowship, for we are all catholics in the sense that we are universally in Christ across the world.

What we are seeing is a mass exodus from the church, particularly in identity. In my observations, it appears that people are becoming non-affiliated with Roman Catholics, Eastern Orthodox, and Protestant denominations alike. I find this reasonable, given that the people are coming out of a great deception, the American-made charismatics that have destroyed our blessed faith, and the religious authoritarians who have used it to oppress the rest.

In short, you both look like phonies, and the only way we will know who is actual, who goes through the strait gate, the narrow is the way, is by becoming more biblical. The church is in a reformational transition back to the basics of our faith, meeting in houses (Acts 2:46, 5:42). The remnant is shrinking, and those who truly want to follow Jesus are being forced out of cathedrals, temples, and other buildings. Alas, this forces us to ask: What is the church? Which is more important: the building we call a church, or the people? Must we enter a building on Sunday and Wednesday to be saved? If so, do we find a contradiction? Ideally, we would gather daily, not once a week, wherever and whenever, exhorting one another so that we might continue (Hebrews 3:13). The building we call a church is a *congregation* point, meaning that the body comes together to fellowship, worship, and learn there. Still, it can be anything: a home, a temple (Acts 2:46-47), or a mountaintop (Matthew 5-7), but the important point is that the congregation is wherever the body comes together in His name.

That does not mean we lack decency and order. That is biblical, as are the ministerial gifts within the congregation, which assembles most commonly in a building. This is where we can learn about God through our biblical ministers, edifying the body by teaching, praying, and pastoring, as we are all guided by the Holy Spirit, whom we all have and should therefore check with scripture in our independent studies. Therefore, to be a part of God's program, you must follow His Gospel gate through the Word of God first, and recognize the helpfulness of the evangelists, teachers, and pastors, made possible by the prophets and apostles before them.

This ministry is not confined to a building topped with a cross, but is everywhere where there may be an evangelist, teacher, and leader in any public place. Still, we can be relatively certain you will find these gifts within the cross-topped establishment. That said, perhaps we should consider whether the church we attend is topped with a cross or an American flag; if we would be better off fellowshipping, worshipping, and studying among a small, select group at home rather than among the American-made system.

To push back on potential destruction, it's important to note that biblical tutors and governors are a good, even necessary thing. Above all, we should want to submit to God's Word and go out of our way to learn how to properly exegete the passage so that we may all be students of the Holy Spirit. This may be the American church's only hope, as course correction on an institutional scale may be a vain feat considering the corruption that has crept in.

Still, by faith, the remnant will overcome.

From there, it is given unto some the excitement of the evangelist, the knowledge of the teacher, the shepherding of the pastor, particularly in groups of two or three when it comes to elders. Therefore, we *must* go to church, and to that end, we *must* find a church that follows God's word, not by our leading but by the leading of the Holy Spirit, who, when sought in sincere, fervent prayer, will answer, if we are to survive. That may look diverse, and is not limited to a certain day. Go to church as often as possible to nourish your spiritual body. I know we can feed our spirit in different ways, but neglecting fellowship and the spiritual assembly thereof can bring great harm, and arguably prove how false our proclamation of faith was.

To survive, we *must* have fellowship, a shepherd, and doctrine. I caution you, my beloved: do not believe your mental understanding alone is enough to sustain your Spirit. Faith alone is, and faith produces fellowship, among many other fruits. Wide is the path to destruction, and that path is filled with false doctrines, false christs, false gospels, and false prophets. This is how millions are deceived daily.

Be found by God where he is today, in his body of believers.

The Good Man Wins

      There is an old saying, a proverb, that goes, "Nice guys finish last." This is a familiar saying that many men, often in pain and suffering, have taken to heart as a dagger, stopping their hearts minute after minute until they no longer beat. However, upon examining the proverb more closely and comparing it with the Word, I have found that this saying conveys positivity, encouragement, and strength in Christ, despite its inherent negativity and connotations.

      Darkness is present only when light is not, meaning a negative can be a positive depending on an individual's mindset. Mirroring: We hold the power to bring light to the dark, just as we can turn a positive into a negative. You, the good man (here, being interchanged with nice), how are you proverbially "good?" Is it by your own accord? To some, their definition of good is backed by Man's definitions and manipulations of the term in its absolute. It is not a matter of characteristics and actions alone, but is determined based on God's nature, measurable in His Word. Therefore, the good man does what is right and follows his Master's word, not what is morally perceived or indignantly self-righteous.

      So the last will be first, and the first last.
— Matthew 20:16 (ESV)

In all ways, the world's value system runs counterclockwise to God's. When examining why someone is "good," we often simplify it to materialistic or arbitrary things, primarily based on preference. Our mental conception of things will produce an interesting twist for many of us when we enter the presence of the Lord in Heaven: those who are esteemed and respected in this life for their wealth, preferential treatment, or compromise on Christ will be frowned upon by God. Yet, for the nice guy, we have hope in understanding that the opposite is also true, that those who are despised and rejected in this life will be rewarded by God in the next.

We would err to believe that our arbitrary means of secular rankings would be a justifiable reason to be disheartened by what the world deems "worthless," among other choice words. I offer you a new parable: the good man who loses the world will gain eternal life (Mark 8:36), the *real* victory that the world will not see and does not desire. Thus, another manipulation of the term is solidified by the matriarchs of Man to the men who will listen, but are shattered by the one who does not stand on Man's municipalities but on God's word. Yes, the world offers riches, power, and beauty beyond compare, which is the same deception that the Devil used initially, as that old serpent.

What are riches? What attains power? What garners beauty? Not all deceptions shine and glimmer like gold, but they come in the form of false brotherhood with the darkness of mankind. Thus, as men and women of God, we must ask ourselves if the partner we seek to purchase with our pearls is a member in Christ or the flesh — a spouse or a swine.

Understand that this is not said to bring offense but rather to reveal the importance of valuing what blessings God has given us, the same as you, being the most important of these, which is a spouse. To the unmarried, a Godly relationship may be a beautiful thing. To the man whose ministry is marriage, a wife is the best gift he can receive from God outside of his salvation, for she is valued *far* above rubies. Therefore, to him, the importance of being one with Christ Jesus and recognizing his value as a son of God is tremendously important, as is the value she would find in the same. She who was purchased by the blood of Jesus should be sought to be purchased by the pearls that match the value of the rubies, deserved by he who appreciates them and not the swine who savors slop.

Now, to the swine, who may not recognize their nature, thinking they speak when they oink and smell of sweet savor when they are a stench in the nostrils of the Lord: the pig does not recognize its nature, for it is not drawn to its recognition nor self-awareness but to the things it desires, being baths in the mire, lounging in the sun, and gobbling garbage. Mirroring, the swine does not identify with Christ but with the world's values, opinions, beliefs, and ways. Therefore, when the sow sees a good, godly individual, it does not value them for what they are worth, what materialistic items they have, nor who they are in Christ Jesus, and the character thereof, but for what they look like, what compromises they are willing to make, and their similarity in nature. When these standards are absent, the same person is "pitied" when they play the pigs game until the game becomes boring and the "bad" boy or girl manifests. In other words, when seeing a partner, do not seek the approval of one who likes the world, but one of God:

> They are from the world; therefore, they speak from the world, and the world listens to them. We are from God. Whoever knows God listens to us; whoever is not from God does not listen to us. By this we know the Spirit of truth and the spirit of error.
> — 1 John 4:5-6 (ESV)

Now, we know the Spirit of Truth and the nature of error — the identified will be identified, regardless of their self-proclaimed affiliation, by their fruits, if nothing else. Friends, do not waste your time on prospects who propagate negativity rooted in contrary beliefs, but spend your time on the things of God, and let *Him* provide you with a Godly, Holy Spirit-filled believer who will come to you when you least expect it. Your time is God's time, and His time, which is now, is always perfect. This perfection will be personified in the one brought to you, for we are made perfect in Christ by accepting the purchasing power of his blood.

To this end, I say, to those of you who are in pain and suffering due to the ill-identification and misplacement of value, both yourself and your romantic pursuits, let Christ be your relief. Let your suffering be with him, for though we are called to suffer, it is for Christ's sake, not our own. Thus, let us not permissively suffer. That can be avoided by walking in his perfect will, understanding all written in His word by the selfsame Spirit.

The Expected End

I hope this letter inspires, comforts, and gives you hope.

In my recent wanderings across the digital landscape, I have witnessed a great deal of fear being spread by believers and non-believers alike. Yay, the populace looks to the heavens and sees the signs, not being inspired but *terrified*. The non-believer gazes, unable to ignore the "coincidences" of prophecy, slowly but surely being fulfilled. Then, a worse thought eclipses the believers, for they do not see the signs and visualize vindication, saying, "Behold, the bridegroom cometh," but instead see their demise and claim they know the day that will bring it.

I do not see the body of Jesus Christ, nor the bride, but the defeatist and the fearful.

This, by no means, is an acceptable representation of our Lord, for we are not defeated but have overcome through Him who already has and *should be* living within us by our confession and faith. We do not have a fear *of* the Lord, which is to say we have a deep reverence, but fear him because of the thoughts that we listen to that are not His. Thus, the counterfeit believer fear mongers, removing all hope without restoring it, for the spirit they go forward with is not the Spirit of God, which is love, but a spirit of fear, which has the foundation of hate or selfishness. Thus, I protest your ministry, for it is not a message of peace, joy, or hope but, on the contrary, which is, by definition, not of God, but a ministry of terror, sadness, and hopelessness.

> For I know the plans I have for you, declares the LORD, plans for welfare and not for evil, to give you a future and a hope.
> — Jeremiah 29:11 (ESV)

Though the fear of the Lord is the beginning of wisdom, as the Psalmist states, the fear *these* people conjure fails to establish our reverence for our Savior; instead, it puts it in them. In this, we know that any signs in the heavens should not induce a state of peril, but of peace in the promise made to the believer, and if there are any among us who use that to obtain some form of fear-mongering allegiance, they should be marked and avoided.

No man knows the day nor the hour. Anyone who claims otherwise is deceiving you, more than likely for personal gain.

The key to being a *true* believer is that he has received the revelation, the truth of Christ our Lord, by faith. The rest do not. The redeemed are those for whom the Bridegroom cometh to give us an expected end. The unsaved do not see this, for they do not end but continue, unrighteously drinking the blood of Jesus Christ in their communion with him, rendering its power in their lives and those they encounter of no effect. Now, you see the danger of such mentalities and spirits, for they are *all* connected.

So many times, we find the faithful obsessed with the final coming of Christ but not with the Lord himself. They doom and condemn the world, not having the life of Christ, which is the Holy Ghost, within them, but a religious spirit that is self-destructive and damaging, even deadly to those who are caught in its detonation blast. The believer should be obsessed with the Lord — in love with Him, producing life and providing hope in hopeless times.

This is why we testify of what is to come by faith in God's Word.

The question becomes, "If we are analogous 'prophets,' to whom are we sent?" According to His words written in the book of Jeremiah? Babylon. America is Babylon, the same as any nation that has rejected God, worshipping idols, and relishing in wickedness. We are the poets sent to them, the ones who are left. We are sent to aid those who are in the world so they may return to their Spiritual One, which is in the kingdom of heaven, revealed by the Word of God and made accessible by Christ's finished work.

To that end, I ask if *we* have ended, for we cannot be one with God if we actively separate ourselves from Him. This separation is found in the absence of the new birth; we can only be sons and daughters of God if we have been born of His spirit, the same as my mother is my mother, and my father my father, and I their son, because I came from *her* womb and *his* seed.

Are you born of God, or are you still of the flesh? Are you Abraham's seed or the Serpent's seed?

This is an important question you *must* answer, for the answer is a matter of life and death; in this answer, we find the life that is Jesus Christ and the death that is sin, which is the Devil, given in disobedience. Many may live and die in the flesh, listening to the lustful allures of Lucifer. In contrast, few will live in the flesh and die to it, constituting a new birth.

The evidence of the epistles makes this clear — even the requirement placed by God's command, saying we *must* be born again, adds to this. Do not ignore the Lord thy God, who has said this to *you*. We are justified by faith, meaning we are justified freely by our faith in God, Jesus Christ. We are cleansed by the purchasing power of His blood and given inheritance through the seal of the Holy Spirit, awaiting redemption.

This is how God produces born-again believers.

Still, it's asked, "What relevance does this have to the end of the world?" I say, "Everything," while the unsaved say, "Nothing." To elaborate, when thinking about worlds, the most important one that requires your concern is your own, first, and your brothers and sisters, second, gaining priority after receiving the Holy Spirit. *Then* the Lord will ask, "What have you done since you have received the Holy Ghost?"

Having heard and followed, we are ready for service.

We are sent to the world to preach the Gospel, to share the life-changing, life-saving power of the cross. This is the commission, but instead of doing our

duty, we cower behind our screens, spreading fear in Satan's supplication rather than comfort in fellowship with our brothers and sisters.

Test the spirits.

Satan's thoughts toward you are thoughts of stress and evil, encouraging you not to end but to continue in comfort and take refuge in your religion.

Religion is not enough. If your refuge is in your works and not in the reason for the works, then you are a lost cause.

Being conceptually "saved" alone is not enough. This repetition is not redundant but intentional. Those who profess their religion but whose profession is based on fallacy or is not legitimate do not receive eternal life, whereas the truly saved have both a profession of faith and possession by God, having read and accepted, heard and followed the Word of the Lord.

That said, I pose a question: What is more common, the end of our world or the world we live in? Millions die in the flesh daily, yet the world remains. Thus, it is the end of our world, and the worlds around us, that are more common and should be our *top* priority. Furthering the thought, I ask, "What is more known between the two worlds? No man knows the day or hour, but we know death is the great equalizer. To that end, we don't know when we will die, for God may take us tomorrow or in twenty years, but He will take us nonetheless. Thus, again, the priority is not to "best guess" the coming of the Lord but to know through faith (which inevitably takes on the mind of Christ) that the Lord cometh to give us an expected end *today*.

Now is your time with God; your opportunity to become regenerated by the Regenerator is present. I pray that you now see, not retaining your blindness, chosen or predestined. You must ask and answer these questions here, receiving your pardon from judgment of God, before inevitably being found guilty before His throne when we all go to give our answer.

Who are you? Do you wear a wedding garment? Has our Lord given you an expected end? Do you take the life you've been given to the lost in Babylon or condemn them selfishly, harboring eternal life like a glutton who can never be satiated though his cup overflows? Some of us are not herders but hoarders; joyless and not joyful, fearful and not fearless, dead and not alive. We do not fish for men but eat them until their grease flows down our cheeks, destroying them far before we offer deliverance. What is this wicked and adulterous generation — you who seek signs and wonders? We are worshippers of the sun and moon, far before we are true worshippers of Christ. We are Babylonians, far before we are Christians.

Who is the I AM to you? A peer, prophet, or Savior? Judgment, deceiver, or deliverance? Yes, we behold that the Bridegroom cometh, but have you asked yourself if He comes for you? Do you know His thoughts toward *you*? Do you have peace in times of peril?

There is still time, and even following the eclipse, I believe there will still be, for mercy is still present. This is your hope, believers, and not. The God of Hope is alive, and with His promise, we believe He will not leave you nor forsake you. *These* are words of life, and if you accept them, you will attain them. Don't run to the applications; run to the Lord. Don't run to the people who preach cultish, doomsday doctrine, but to your Lord, and receive the Holy Spirit through prayer and *true* repentance, not alone, but among pastors and peers. This is repentance: a complete turning away from your sin and turning to the cross instead, with your mind and purpose changed by a good conscience toward God. Do not turn away from *Him*. Do not turn back to the old ways after experiencing Him. Go to the cross and cling to Jesus until He comes, knowing that He shall never let you go. His Word — the Holy Spirit — will seal you as the born-again Christian you were predestinated to be.

Repent and bear witness to the kingdom of heaven at hand.

look upon the stars and see His glory
see the celestial bodies and wonder
what is man that He would think of us
these thoughts of our expected end
provided by the love of God exclusively
are what He thinks toward us now and
what He thought for all
eternity

The Clause of Nuclear Hopelessness

I have seen many faces, each in many colors, shapes, and sizes, with different features. *This* exemplifies God's perfection in His masterwork, the individual, the art piece of the Lord, whom we call people. Despite their differences, I have noticed a commonality that becomes more apparent as the days go by. This is no surprise given the days we're living in, but even still, its growth is rapid, alarming, saddening, and consistent.

This commonality is called "hopelessness," and anybody who has walked this earth past the season of accountability knows the feeling. Even the predestined have felt hopelessness or may feel it one day. I know this because of the certainty in the implication made by God's word:

> May the God of hope fill you with all joy and peace in believing, so that by the power of the Holy Spirit you may abound in hope.
> — Romans 15:13 (ESV)

Not placing the cart before the horse, we examine the clause of nuclear hopelessness, which is phrased this way to bring attention to the Creator who thought of us before the foundation of the world. Now we know that we, whom God has chosen, agreed to choose Him in return, regardless of the suffering we would incur and have incurred, for the sake of our Lord Jesus Christ. However, the term "nuclear hopelessness" should be explored in the clause, for it is both a pun and a promise given our times. Nuclear warheads wait in the waters to wipe out all of humanity in less than an hour. In most conversations, nuclear verbiage is commonplace and on the tip of our tongues, like the "big red buttons" are at the tips of our world leaders' fingers. This is only one of many contributors to the hopelessness of our time, for what hope have we in mutually assured destruction?

Anxiously, the worries don't end there.

The economy is crashing, the food is poisoning, the governments are toppling, the people are wailing, more are gnashing, wars are devastating, and the believers are scrapping. I have fought hopelessness this year. Left and right, I hear the talks of the return of Christ, which is, on one hand, great and, on the other hand, terrible, depending on your faith. Don't misunderstand me, my brothers and sisters, for as much as any of you, I rejoice at the mention of our Lord's return in the spirit, yet find myself mourning in the flesh. The thought of being taken tomorrow takes me to the visions of what will never be — what is no more, hurling me existentially and inevitably by the passing thought that asks whether or not any of this has worth. If I am to leave this Earth, then to what point is it to pen this prose? If there is no tomorrow, what value do we have for today? I often imagine the invisible audience of futurity as the one I write to, providing purpose for my penning that occasionally seems pointless.

Now, enter the God of Hope.

We are not only fleshy creatures, but also spiritual ones, making us supernaturally aware, for we are born again in the Spirit of God, making Him our Father and us His sons and daughters. With this, we understand that we have passed — we die daily, facing persecution, danger, and the daily sacrifice of our own desires and safety so that we might preach the Gospel. To this end, I ask, "What have we to mourn? We are already dead."

Oh, believers! What work Christ does in us is not worthless; our entire worth is found in Him! Look to the cross; it points to the purpose, the life, and the worship, all done in Spirit and Truth by the *true* worshipper. And tomorrow? We were never promised it; we have it right *now*. God has given us *this:* decreasing tomorrow's value to increase today's purchasing power. If He is to come tomorrow, it is no different than if you were to die today, for both instances are in God's hands, knowing the time for both occasions.

And of the invisible audience? In the kingdom of heaven, a portion of the assembly is *always* invisible. We do not see them; we lack omniscience and omnipresence; that belongs to God alone, not saints or Mary. That aside, we could not possibly fathom the lives God can touch through ours, but they are lives nonetheless. Even in our physical death, the testimony of Jesus Christ can reach millions, for though we may fall, fail, or pass, God's word will never stagger, sink, or perish.

It is eternal.

We do not have a valueless purpose, but one that is in high demand and restored as long as we give our gifts and lives to God. Though the time is minute, the kingdom is vast, and those who give their lives will produce the seed of *their* kind in *their* time, cut short or redeemed. More than this, my precious brothers and sisters, remember the God of Hope, for He remembers you. *He* fills you with all joy and peace, believing that we may abound in hope, through the power of the Holy Ghost that unites the kingdom.

Now, we see that there can not be a God of Hope without hopelessness, for what is an attribute of God without the anti-attribute to draw it out? By this thought, we realize the goodness of the deal and why we signed on the dotted line despite the clause of nuclear hopelessness. There is no sorrow without a plan, weakness without strength, or life without death. Of all these good things mentioned? They are found in Christ Jesus, a haver of many titles, but in this case, the God of Hope.

He is King. *He* is risen. *He* is alive.

Though the world has nuclear weaponry and powers beyond comprehension, we have a power greater than these: the power of the Holy Ghost, which holds all these forces in subjection, the same ones He will loose in His time and by His will, not to the bride's bruising but to the Jezebels' judgment.

Have hope, my people. Have faith. The kingdom of heaven is at hand, and it is in and around everyone who is called according to his purpose.

Generation of Fools

*W*e live in dangerous times.

The devil's wiles have taken hold through his finite knowledge, enough to deceive the masses despite their lack of completeness. Most believers, unlike, support antichrist dogmas, doctrines, and politics. They are blinded by their hubris and made foolish by their intelligence. They are oppressed by demons who call themselves Christ and can complete the heist due to the individuals' incomplete revelation.

Those who *know* Christ even once believe in Christ, indeed. Those who comprehend Christ alone have never known him and still do not know him.

Oh, you Gentiles, as blind as the Jews that were made so for your sake! You persecute Christ in his people and symbolically crucify them. In the same public manner, the same as the Pharisees before you and the haters of Noah and Abraham before them, you, the self-proclaimed Keepers of the Law and Hoarders of Knowledge, seek yourselves far before you seek God. You push your politics far before your praise. You persecute rather than bring peace. You are putrid in the nostrils of the Lord when you disgrace your faith, representing Satan while being a worshipper of his ways.

The worst of it all is that you don't see it.

Prepare yourself, true believer. Activate your faith. It's only going to get harder to hear from here. I am not ignorant of the slew of laws being passed in America, and I am not naive to the wickedness of this nation. America, you Babylonians — worshippers of gods and idols, and lovers of sin, getting drunk off the blood of the martyrs, the saints: *your time is nigh*. All of Hell moves against you to shift the balance into the hands of the antichrist. There is a spiritual invasion that has taken hold of the actual country of this nation, which is the people who have aligned with the coming Devilman, the same as you. *You,* country of warmongers, adulterers, pedophiles, and sacrificers, and all other forms of wickedness, are *terrorizers,* much like the Christians and correct politics you come against.

It is all *wicked!* Man is wicked. His laws are wicked. Yet, you'd sooner align with the communists and terrorists before the Lord? You drive the American people and, to an extent, the world into the hands of the beguiler. The New World Order comes, and it is a world run by the antichrist. His spirit has established authority in position to the degree that the majority of you would align yourself with a bear of propaganda before a man of God.

Do not be quick to anger, the same way I have not. I have received righteous indignation in my long-suffering due to ignorance, arrogance, and general tomfoolery.

The propaganda of a man versus a bear has framed the entirety of men as a demon, using horrid experiences that, though valid and worthy of discussion, do not justify such hatred. You do not create solutions with your propaganda, but multiply the problems. You lead hundreds of thousands to their deaths, not caring for the well-being of your fellow man, but harmful, wicked, and deadly politics by contributing to the spiritual death of multitudes, the cultivation of hate, and the insanity that is pseudo-intellectualism, which has made you *dumb*. These are the same entities that entice men into taking their lives rather than being attacked by them.

Yet, you continue in your ways, unbothered and unchanging? How can you live with such results?

Understand me: I am empathetic to the horrors of the world and understand what men *and* women have done to women *and* men. I understand the hypothetical question of choosing the man or the bear's intended meaning. Still, I have an issue with the phrasing: Whether one should choose the man or the bear is irrelevant when the question is hateful propaganda by definition, and ill-thought-out. It's akin to the rest of the world's politics: the foolish riding the mass wave of fools, which is and will be, for a short while, the principalities in high places. Their objective has been evident for years, first manifesting itself in feminism, then the destruction of gender roles, followed by the sexual revolution, and now the corruption of the democratic and republican systems.

I say all this passively to imply that, in my opinion, this is all part of an agenda with a clear anti-Christ through line, promoting politics that directly dismiss and combat God's, in some capacities, in fascistic or communist ways, particularly in churning out propaganda.

Man, in simple terms, is an animal. Without God? Even more so. The godless nations have made this clear, proving that Man is not worse than a bear but equal to its animalistic nature, which is savage, brutal, and, though kind to degrees, a predator at its heart. Regardless of whichever you choose, you will be mauled, and in certain cases (though less so), you can say the same thing about women. The only safe choice is a man of God who can draw both into his subjection through Jesus Christ.

I must address the women to elaborate on my views on this political matter because they have twisted God's word so they may mold it into the image of their politics. In all honesty, this is the entire purpose of writing this prose; up until this point, it didn't phase me too much. Foolish propaganda is only believed by fools; I couldn't care less. But twisting God's Word to fit an agenda does spark a fire in me. You who make a false teacher of yourself, having lent your ear to the spirit of the antichrist to demonize men by the Bible. You lead yourself and millions of others to the pits of Hell, which is the just reward for those who listen to demonic voices rather than the Word of God.

Know where you stand with the Lord, who leads us all.

We were once equal, perfectly placed in the program of God in the time of Eden, but since Man's fall, an established order in God's word must be followed. There are checks and balances, but one sure thing is that you follow God's word, which must be read by the Spirit of God, which only dwells in those who are cleansed, consecrated, and holy by faith in the finished work of the cross.

Based on your fruits alone, I can, in good judgment, see why you do not understand what God is saying.

Humble yourselves. You are church reign-takers who lead your people to desolation, standing behind the pulpit, pastoring and preaching while you willfully ignore God's command not to do so in ill will, not exemplifying Christ but instead desiring the power that was not given to you. Like Jezebel, those of us who unrighteously obtain power will immodestly try to get the world's attention to our downfall.

> I say this to help you, though many of you will not see it.
> Let a man meet a she-bear robbed of her cubs
> rather than a fool in his folly.
> — Proverbs 17:12 (ESV)

The above passage is the scripture that many women who hate men have quoted to justify their hatred for them. Despite the emphasis on gender, this does not mean it is *exclusive* to men alone. Many scriptures are directed to men, and some are gender exclusive, read to all men, but all people, male and female, Jew and Gentile, and diverse races must take this scripture to heart. Thus, by the placement of the scriptures, *anyone* who despises the wisdom and instruction of God is a *fool* and should be avoided.

Who despises the wisdom and instructions of God more than someone who hates men for simply being men?

> The fear of the LORD is the beginning of wisdom,
> and the knowledge of the Holy One is insight.
> — Proverbs 9:10 (ESV)

Fear the Lord!
This is to say to *respect* the Word you spit and step on.

Blind believers: rebuke the devils that have you bound. Know that while God moves, the Devil does, too. With every dollar, there is a counterfeit, only made visible to those who have the original print, which is the Word of God. Go to the touchstone to test the plate metal to know whether or not what you say is true.

Politics is wicked when it is of this world, of Man. It can be the counterfeit, the archetype of the fallen world to come, not the New Earth that the redeemed shall inherit —that you should desire to be with, not the loser Lucifer. If we apply politics biblically, letting God's law and kingdom be our judicial standard, then we are at ease. But when you want to be communists and not Christians, antisemites and not ambassadors, politicians and not parables, you do not know the Lord, and he *will* say to you those words that you all so faithlessly fear:

And then will I declare to them, "I never knew you; depart from me, you workers of lawlessness."
— Matthew 7:23 (ESV)

Repent. Turn away from the wisdom of man, my people!

America, I pray you know God by His mercy rather than His wrath. Either way, you *will* come to know God. The scriptures are being fulfilled, and you all, doers of good and evil, are their enactors.

May God have mercy on us all.

The Importance of the Holy Ghost

𝔄n address to the jaded believer,

I understand the hardships and weight of being a representative of Christ, not only in the social regard but also in the spiritual, prophetically promised, and previously spoken of in God's word. Like me, I'm sure you understand my referencing of the scriptures and how their fulfillment does not come as a surprise but is assuring. In this blessed assurance, we have hope, knowing what will come and who will be there when it does:

> May the God of hope fill you with all joy and peace in believing, so that by the power of the Holy Spirit you may abound in hope.
> — Romans 15:13 (ESV)

Stipulating this only implies a coming juxtaposition, a recurring theme for me, as I'm sure you've noticed upon reading this text. So, let me explore the juxtaposition, not to your embarrassment or to provoke you into anger, but to help you potentially prevent a coming outcome that will damage you and those who can be saved, and refuse to be saved. In fairness, the flesh finds it impossible to deal with spiritual things when it is without its Spiritual Cure. We're no different from the Jews of old, in that regard, who did not have access to the Holy Spirit given Christ's yet-to-be-fulfilled coming and, therefore, could not be made perfect. In their flesh, as many stories show, they failed *repeatedly*. King David fell short due to the desires of his flesh, causing him to send Bathsheba's husband to the front lines of war so that he might take her as his wife upon her husband's inevitable passing. He paid *dearly* for this act, as Moses did when he was not permitted to enter the promised land due to his lack of temperament, causing him to disobey God's command — His word, to speak to the rock and not smite it upon the children of Israel's second need for water. Even Abraham, the father of the faith, backslid due to his fleshy fear, nearly causing death to befall Pharaoh and, to an extent, all of Egypt.

If it weren't for God's intervention, Abraham would have been made a murderer.

The point is that we will fail in our flesh; this is another assurance. If we walk in the flesh, we will fall in the flesh, for the flesh, by nature, is fallen, sinful, and iniquitous. It is only in walking in the Spirit that we will understand, though we fall, He has overcome. Knowing that God is the Spirit, we understand that it is a *necessity* that we walk with Him in the way He tells us: By faith apart from works, so that works may proceed by faith.

Even the Jews, having faith, repented and were saved, for it was not in their following of the law that saved them, but in their faith in the coming Messiah, who would one day be the perfect sacrifice.

In His endless love, the Lord desires a personal fellowship with us. The relationship, personally and individually attained, brings us into His unified, spiritual body. I say that to say this: even with the Spirit of God within you, you *will* fail, and in my best judgment, according to scripture, your failure is *imminent*, but without it, you will fail *utterly*. There would be no sense of urgency to this if I did not believe the issue was immediate, but after watching you, as millions of others do, I have been inspired by your urgency. I see a coming short-falling that will do more damage than the current bursts, like a breaking dam with the cracks present and leaking, presiding over a town of millions, ready to wipe it out when the weight of the water can no longer be borne.

I have seen an unrighteous anger fall upon you, not toward the Devil (which is where it should be placed), but toward the people. I have no issue with righteous indignation, but this is the furthest thing from it. For example, when a brother or non-believer disagrees with you, the immediate reaction should not be physical violence or even the thought of it, but a loving, controlled, and patient one. We know these battles we fight are not flesh and blood affairs but spiritual ones, and the Spirit of God is not an anger-inducing or provoking one but one of peace and joy.

I see your joy and peace fleeting.

Your vocabulary gets more frustrated, offensive, and worldly with every address to your followers. Worst of all, you are blind to your backslidings and consider them justified. Your blind justification could lead you and millions of others to a physical war that God will hold you responsible for. With love, I will identify the origin of your issue so that you may choose to let God remove it. Otherwise, you will keep it in your heart.

As the apostle Paul states, our weaknesses are our strengths. Your greatest strength, your intellect, is also your greatest weakness. With God, your knowledge is a powerful tool essential to the Kingdom of Heaven. You can do great good as a teacher, evangelist, or pastor with God's knowledge. I have seen you do this and give roses where they are due; I have learned much from your gift.

I thank God for it and you.

Your ability to confront the devil's lies today is unmatched, undefeated, and indisputable. That is why the Devil does not aim to face you intellectually but spiritually, on scriptural grounds. Thus, he turns the scripture into a blindfold, using your wits against you, throwing constant adversary after adversary to tire you out, hitting you in the spirit, which you cannot see, while distracting you with the imps he knows will annoy you. This is possible when you are not a prisoner of Christ but a prisoner of your mind, created by the twisting of the Word like heated metal, making your hardened steel prison.

This is the Devil's chosen battleground: the mind. Logic and reason are his greatest assets, though in his usage, they are for twisting.

The modern Christian believes that their intellect will save them. Still, they fail to remember that the devil is the greatest intellectual there is and that salvation does not come by knowledge alone but by the blood of Jesus, only acceptable by faith. Unrighteous reason will only lead to the demonic destruction of your soul. Demons deceive, and often they will use our emotions, imaginations, and fleshy desires to harm us, to have access to our souls, either owned by God or by the Devil. Depending on the spirit, we either believe or do not, and that determines who will take us for eternity.

As leaders of the people, your faith or faithlessness is not only sought by both sides but is *vital* to the people's aid or detriment. Therefore, we know what the most critical mind must be: the mind of Christ. Many believe that the mind of Christ means conceiving him in the brain, but based on the previous understanding, we know that the conception of Christ does not occur in the cortex alone, but in the heart. God has said He desires to be in our hearts, and for God to be there, our temple, which is our body, we must accept His cleansing blood. What dwells in the heart is welcomed by either faith or doubt, not knowledge, intellectualism, or theological prestige (though all have their places), but by belief or unbelief alone.

Who has your mind? Who has your heart? The results should be shown in your actions and inactions while the world is watching. If Christ is in the heart, your spirit and body are his to control. However, he can only be in control if you give him complete dominion over your life — make Him your Lord. This is therefore the expansion of the vindication of the justified: Scripture alone is the claim to our faith, and has clear instructions on how that faith is "justified" in James's sense:

> You see that faith was active along with his works, and faith was completed by his works; and the Scripture was fulfilled that says, "Abraham believed God, and it was counted to him as righteousness"—and he was called a friend of God. You see that a person is justified by works and not by faith alone.
> — James 2:22-24 (ESV)

Justified here is δικαιοῦται (dikaioutai), a present passive indicative verb meaning "is shown to be righteous," "vindicated," or "declared just," that our works prove the authenticity of our faith. Still, it is not the constitution of the legal basis for our salvation. Essentially, if we look at the context of James earlier, it clearly states that this is shown to "someone," meaning it is before men, not God.

> But someone will say, "You have faith and I have works." Show me your faith apart from your works, and I will show you my faith by my works.
> — James 2:18 (ESV)

Abraham was justified before God (Genesis 15:6), far before he was justified before men (Genesis 22:1-18), presenting the evidence, the vindication of a faith and righteousness that had already been established decades before. Therefore, those who open the Scripture and believe it will live it as sons and daughters of God who do the works out of love, knowing that we are justified before God forever. We are His servants to this generation, and if you believe God is eternal, then what was said to Abraham, shown to Moses and David, solidified by Elijah, declared by John the Baptist, taken the form of Jesus, and later explained by Paul, is for you, if you are willing to accept it.

Not them alone. *You.*

The Great Commission proves this and encourages us to do what some of our brothers would call "heretical." We work so that our light may shine before men, so that our good works would glorify our Father (Matthew 5:16). Let the naysayers say what they will, but I say what God said: do it all in the Spirit of God. It has fallen to us to be His representatives.

Due to your gifts, you have been raised. The question is: who has raised you? Whom do you work for? Without the Holy Ghost, your anger, frustration, impatience, and misleadings will only worsen, as anyone else would following in the footsteps of a bad master. With the Holy Ghost, you will have patience, joy, and Hope, among many other things that are spiritually given. Either way, the human being is a spiritual creature. You *will* have a spirit, clean or unclean. That is why I write to encourage you to have the Spirit of God, which has been called the Holy Spirit and the Holy Ghost, not only to help you fight the spirits you already do, but so that you may be sealed unto your day of redemption, not losing your soul in your fight against the spirits that attack. This can only be done through your spiritual birth of God, which is how we are given our inheritance, our promise of Abraham.

With this sacrifice of your life, you will do greater things for your people than you could imagine, which is what I would love to see for you. What you are doing now is good, but with the proper spirit, it could be life-changing. Without the appropriate spirit, it will end in destruction. What you have, being intelligent, is a gift of God. Use it for Him, by Him, according to His word.

Being gifted in this manner is both fortunate and unfortunate. You are held to a harsher standard than most and must rise to that standard by God's grace. It is an honor and a burden, a blessing and a curse. The difference is the body you walk in, for gifts and callings come without repentance. If we walk in the body of Christ, we do not face these challenges alone. In the flesh, we are alone, even dead, though we walk without knowing it.

With love and encouragement, your brother,

John Anderson

A Word Unto Men

My friends in and out of the body of Christ,

I'm writing today with a message to a fearful world. It does not take a genius, Christian, or worldly man to recognize that this world is falling apart. Daily, we near an end that will surely come. As a generation united by our placement in time, we have the responsibility and dissatisfaction of watching it unfold into chaos. We cannot change what *will* happen; we can only make a *difference*.

Be watchful, stand firm in the faith, act like men, be strong.
— 1 Corinthians 16:13 (ESV)

What makes us different from others, in a simple way of thinking, is our response to stressful situations. Many Christians believe that what makes them different from the rest is that God will come to their rescue, preventing them from going through persecution or trials. However, this is not promised; for everything there is a time and a season for all things under heaven (Ecclesiastes 3:1-8). We must be ready to act appropriately in each situation and understand every action, post-action, and correction. So again, we see what makes believers different is the God-given *response*, the *actions* taken to meet the circumstances

or challenges of the day in which they are placed. When a sickness falls upon a worldly person, their immediate response is fear, which is understandable given that they have no hope for what befalls them when they die, nor that a God of miracles might heal them, or even provide wisdom for a practical healing. They fear death, and when a genuine and sometimes visible threat is made, they turn their anger toward varying victims. At the same time, hopelessness sets in due to the uncertainty of the situation.

This is ironic, given how much trust an unbeliever places in their science. If it is so perfect and infallible, why do you fear the diseases you claim to have cures for? Is it perhaps because the practice of science is fallible, has no long-term guarantee, and is only their best hope, which is why this world has no hope at all in its man-made form? The science of this world, medicine, is not only fallible but bought and paid for by the corporations that support other corporations. It is not used solely to make people better but to fight sickness with sickness, fire with fire, and burn every member of this country to the ground so they might inherit their small portion of the wealth produced from its ecological succession, in my opinion.

This is not to say that all medicine is bad, but that this is allegorically why secularism does not provide invincible hope for the average person: Science changes. Medicine changes. Regardless, we all die.

Medicine and science have their purpose and practice in the kingdom of God, and the self-evident truth of life is that there will inevitably be death. In the grand examination of medicine, in the context of human longevity, it is an expensive band-aid that Man has patented and trademarked as a cure-all for the incurable. It has the slyest sales pitch and the most manipulative showmanship: take me or embrace the infinite, the "nothingness" that comes after.

In other cases, medicine can improve our quality of life, but it will never prevent our inevitable outcome. Medicine and science cannot save you; they are not meant to. Like everything else in a capitalist country, they exist to make money and hopefully help a few people along the way. However, they are among the most profitable business models in the States, grossing billions of dollars annually as of 2022. This is because they have a captive audience and repeat customers, attained by fear and contradiction, absorbing the mass market in a deadly niche, similar to the prosperity healer who uses miracles in the same capacity.

This industry has only one major competitor: God.

This competition is evident in His children, for believers do not fear but have peace, joy, hope, and certainty when sickness occurs. We have peace in knowing that God has promised us practical and supernatural means of being healed, if God wills. We also have blessed assurance in our eternal preservation, so that if we do pass on, we know we go to be directly in the presence of our Lord Jesus (2 Corinthians 5:8). In all things, death and life, sickness and healing, we give glory to God who can turn even the most unfortunate of circumstances into a beautiful testimony of His goodness.

This is one of many reasons science and its overlords hate and diametrically oppose God's Word. They did not once; it is a shame they have fallen away, having never believed to begin with. Science, once the method for testing the established truth of God's creation, is now a tool used to test its own, constantly shifting theories that hold no ground in their hypothetical stasis. Worse, it is used to *disprove* God (though they fail) primarily because He is the only one capable of challenging them in any real sense. I find this ironic, given that God can use medicine to do His will. Medicine can aid the body's natural processes, and God is more than okay with such practical means. Human bodies and all portions of nature contain intelligence that instructs them to produce life and repair it when damage or sickness comes.

That intelligence is a creation of God, and medicine can absolutely facilitate this process, even aid it, to healing by the Healer.

In all this, we see that the lost respond with unbelief, not only in God but eventually in Man as well. The believer responds with faith in God, understanding His unlimited power inside and outside Man. You can apply this same study to all characters, and in the end, you will see that what makes a Christian is not their self-proclaimed title but their response to circumstances, for in that response, you can see who God truly knows. Every action will have an equal and opposite reaction, which will determine the production, which, to a believer, should be scripturally identifiable fruits, works, and a precedent for biblical primacy above tradition or ego, among other things.

To what point does any of this relate to being a man? Why bring attention to medicine if the clear thesis is "What maketh Man?" Man is made by faith. A real man walks by it — he has courage, a sound mind, power, and love, does not fear, and has accepted the token of salvation and God, being the blood of Jesus. These are not the characteristics of American men alone, but men of God, though there is an allowance of overlapping seen in the traits naturally placed within the individual, as appealing to the moral law innately placed in all of us. Even then, the strongest American man is the weakest compared to the men in the nation of God. American men will not withstand the terrors of this world, just as no man alone can, which is why the men of God persevere in the face of the adversary, not because they have gender-based, self-made brawn, but because they have found their position in the Lord's host. American-made men will fall, crumble, and panic at the slightest inconvenience. They place their trust in their abilities when, quite simply, they have none that can withstand what is coming; it is not enough. They know this. They fear it, and instead of doing what is best for their family, they go to *those who* can make them able; they foolishly and selfishly turn away and continue to live in fear, doused in alcohol, among other abuses, and enabled by the American dream.

You can take a man of principle who is well-versed in political law, power, and intelligence, and *perceive* that he is fearless. Take away those veils and reveal his true underbelly, and you will quickly watch this man crumble, along with his fallible, nationally founded principles. They know this. They see the end of America is coming, yet they do nothing of any effect.

Mankind has failed constantly throughout its history. This is common knowledge, seen throughout our history of empires, sciences, politics, and powers. The running theme: Man fails; God does not. His word is the only constant throughout human chronology. Despite the many circumstances surrounding the Word, which some use to speak against it, such as time, man's fallibility, the Dead Sea, the King James Council, and the diversity of translations, the Gospel remains intact — the book, perfect. If you disagree, may God help you to see, but if you can be persuaded, I encourage you to examine Him and yourself in His image. Every man must examine what he is made of and what he can do with the character that makes it possible. If you've seen that your character is closely aligned with God, though you may not believe, you are closer and have a better opportunity for salvation than most believing men. If you read this and see that your character aligns more with the world, you are the example I refer to when speaking to non-believers with a better opportunity to know God. To those who believe and see you meet the measure of a believer: *Godspeed.* To those who believe and do not, may the speed of God be granted to you the same, unto your rehabilitation.

Men are meant to have a spine, stand for what's right, and speak *boldly*. Yet I find that the average American woman has more of these qualities than men do. Spineless men (whom I would deem to be the misogynists and cowards) have given way to modern feminism: men acting like women and vice versa, both inside and outside of the church, each growing in more hatred of the other because they have prioritized politics over our principles. What an embarrassment to God's kingdom — a pitiful production of America. My heart grieves for both men and women who mock my worldly nation, of which I am heir, and the onward one that I will return to. All I see these days are cowardly, impressionable, and emasculated men who have succumbed to the powers of this world and will continue to do so lest they give themselves over to the Power that is stronger, eternal, and proven generation after generation.

Act like men, walk like men, talk like men. In the words of God Himself:

Dress for action like a man;
I will question you, and you make it known to me.
— Job 38:3 (ESV)

Your family and the kingdom depend on it. They rely on *you,* who must rely on God.

Eden's Consequence

*A*merican churches,

In my recent travels, I have noticed a relatively harmless argument surrounding the scriptures. However, beneath the mask of inoffensiveness, a wicked devil seeks to mislead a critical revelation. Therefore, as your brother and fellow member of the body of Christ, I write to address this issue and expose the Serpent who hides so expertly in plain sight in religion and politics.

I'm sure, at this point, you understand my stance on many subjects: it is based upon the Word of God. By no means do I intend to mislead you or misguide you, but present God's word as it's presented, not imagining my own "truths," or projecting variations of those as previously done in history, but to display what is *seen*, working with you and not against you, so that we may understand God better.

Cleave to Christ above all else.

Now, without further digression, let us get into an argument, which presents itself in this snide simplicity: Eve cannot be blamed for her fall in the garden, for she did not know what right and wrong were, and Adam, watching, did nothing and was given no blame, though he was solely responsible. This is an argument that is made by a blind believer who is not first a Christian but a feminist, in my opinion. This is no mystery and does not require any tremendous logical leaps to come to such a conclusion, for the offended female rejects the spirit of God and takes on an antichrist spirit to further their agenda rather than the truth. These "Christians" often disguise their politics as religion, made evident in their demonization of men despite our understanding of their completion. Instead of understanding our equitable roles and how we work together, they seek to subvert such expectations and domineer over men, as wicked men before them did.

They become the very monster they hypocritically hate.

Though I agree that both Adam and Eve, male and female, were equal, they are not so now, and were placed that way because of a critical error on both their part.

American feminism is deceptive. Be mindful of its subtlety.

Know ye not that Eve knew the truth? From her tongue, she professed the truth that God gave to Adam, whom He, by extension, gave to Eve. In fairness, the issue is a lack of common sense and critical thinking. The children of God possess both abilities and have learned to read the truth in its apparentness:

> Now the serpent was more crafty than any other beast of the field that the LORD God had made. He said to the woman, "Did God actually say, 'You shall not eat of any tree in the garden'?" And the woman said to the serpent, "We may eat of the fruit of the trees in the garden, but God said, 'You shall not eat of the fruit of the tree that is in the midst of the garden, neither shall you touch it, lest you die.'"
> — Genesis 3:1-4 (ESV)

John the Revelator, in his account of Christ's revelation on the Isle of Patmos, declares the Serpent is Satan (Revelation 12:9). Within this Genesis passage, we can clearly see that Eve confesses her knowledge of the truth to the Serpent, Satan. We also see that the devil is a subtle and cunning creature who knows God's Word better than believers, in that he can twist it to the capacity that it coaxes our egos into disobedience. The Devil's brilliance in this passage is found in his knowledge of the truth and his subtle changing of it with *one word:*

But the serpent said to the woman, "You will not surely die. For God knows that when you eat of it your eyes will be opened, and you will be like God, knowing good and evil."
— Genesis 3:5 (ESV)

This caused Eve to sin, to disobey God, the original sin. She was not ignorant of the truth, but was tempted to believe the Devil when she saw the fruit was good to eat and chose to eat it, relying on her reasoning and understanding rather than God's commands. The better question is, was she alone in this, or did Adam partake also:

So when the woman saw that the tree was good for food, and that it was a delight to the eyes, and that the tree was to be desired to make one wise, she took of its fruit and ate, and she also gave some to her husband who was with her, and he ate. Then the eyes of both were opened, and they knew that they were naked. And they sewed fig leaves together and made themselves loincloths.
— Genesis 3:6-7 (ESV)

Their sinful act and the consequence thereof were far more weighty than we can fathom in our human condition. Not only did the Devil rob Eve of her eternal life, but replaced her equality with equity. This world was Eve's the same way it was Adam's. It was their inheritance, which was only theirs because of God's righteousness imbued in them, being His creation and deriving from His goodness. In this spiritual condition, there was no death, only eternal life. In Adam and Eve's breaking of the first covenant of God, they brought *death* as a *consequence of their actions.*

Hence, the Edenic Covenant (Genesis 2:16-17; Hosea 6:7), a covenant conditional on obedience, was replaced with the Adamic Covenant: one of grace with consequences. In this, we see the truly consequential results of Adam's behavior, for though Eve disobeyed, it was Adam's disobedience that seemed to be weighed more heavily:

And to Adam he said,

"Because you have listened to the voice of your wife
    and have eaten of the tree
of which I commanded you,
    'You shall not eat of it,'

cursed is the ground because of you;
   in pain you shall eat of it all the days of your life;
thorns and thistles it shall bring forth for you;
   and you shall eat the plants of the field.
By the sweat of your face
   you shall eat bread,
till you return to the ground,
   for out of it you were taken;
for you are dust,
   and to dust you shall return."
— Genesis 3:17-19 (ESV)

In comparison to Eve, it's clear that he got the harsher punishment, which, in my theological opinion, shows that his sin was greater:

To the woman, he said,

"I will surely multiply your pain in childbearing;
   in pain you shall bring forth children.
Your desire shall be for your husband,
   and he shall rule over you."
— Genesis 3:16 (ESV)

In the context of Satan, he was told what would become of him by the work of Christ:

The LORD God said to the serpent,

"Because you have done this,
   cursed are you above all livestock
   and above all beasts of the field;
on your belly you shall go,
   and dust you shall eat
   all the days of your life.
I will put enmity between you and the woman,
   and between your offspring and her offspring;
he shall bruise your head,
   and you shall bruise his heel."
— Genesis 3:14-15 (ESV)

Under the Adamic Covenant, we see clear, unconditional principles that outline punishment but set the stage for God's redemptive plan. Alas, in almost humorous irony, Adam blamed Eve (Genesis 3:12), though he partook in the same conception of knowledge. Shortly thereafter, the sacrificial lamb arrived with the new Covenant of Redemption, exemplified by blood, and was placed within a new order, making Adam, the man, the designated ruler over Eve, thereby replacing the harmonious nature of their marriage with a contentious and cursed one. From that point on, the man would be the head of the mother of all living, and we would understand the basics of the Gospel from the protovengelium: Man sins, God judges, and then redeems by His love, grace, and mercy.

This covenant has not changed.

In hindsight, the creation of Adam and Eve paved the way for the fall of man, which in turn paved the way for the plan of redemption, symbolically and typologically displayed in Genesis. Now you see that opposing this doctrine is to go against God's order and plan, placing ourselves above the Husbandman and unrighteously shifting the blame for the consequences. However, I would say it prophetically points to the curse of "desire" described in Genesis 3:16 — the "battle of the sexes," if you will. Alas, feminism has ravaged America, and in its efforts to completely dominate men, they have made men who want to completely dominate women, who are carbon copies of the men before them, who were domineering. These abusive men created domineering, feminist women.

Alas, the cycle of violence.

What a perversion of our minds we have seen, attempting to do the same to the Word of God. She knew the Word as well as Adam, and still listened to the Serpent, first eating the fruit and then giving it to Adam to eat.

The head of the woman is the man; the head of the man is Christ. This is an absolute. However, it would be dishonest to reconcile the clearly outlined conflict as a prophetic outline of what would come, not an instruction manual for how we should mistreat women. As men and women, husbands and wives, there is a mutual submission that reconciles, even redeems, our innate nature and desire to domineer. Perhaps we should be Ephesians, and based on Ephesians 5, remember that our goals as partners are to submit, be godly, and love and respect one another.

I understand women's bitterness toward the fall, for as God declared,

His curse has brought much sorrow, pain, and *death*. I say, "Let us not make a mountain out of a molehill when examining Adam and Eve. If anything, thanks should be to them for making a way for us to come through God's perfect plan of redemption."

On Eve, I find it interesting to note that by her further confession, stating the serpent beguiled her (Genesis 3:13), her consequence was not only solidified for her but for *us*. Now, we live in Satan's stolen world and bear the wages of sin until pardoned, for all of us, due to their disobedience, are born as Caine and Abel were conceived: in sin and iniquity. We are all as guilty as they were, so we should forbear the unproductive judgment of Eve's unchangeable actions. As for Adam's presence in the serpent's beguiling, though plainly seen, should not be discounted; who first believed the Serpent led to Adam sinning, but it was *his* disobedience and his greater understanding of the act that made his punishment more severe. This led to the marriage of the two, sex between Adam and Eve, and the production of their offspring: first Cain and then Abel (Genesis 4:1-2). Intentionally, we see that Cain and Abel both belong to Adam and Eve, not a third party, though some radical counterfeit Christian groups might suggest otherwise.

This is the truth. Let not your emotions or politics precede God's word, for there is much danger in this disobedience and ill-understanding of the scriptures. Go forward in the Spirit of God, knowing your place in His kingdom and to your partner, with all of us being under Christ. Let us focus on being one body comprised of pastors, teachers, and evangelists, as we advance with our theology built upon the backs of the prophets, apostles, and Law, which once were but are no more, in a rather deceptively simple manner of speaking.

Let us have the Holy Spirit, and let this third person of the Trinity be our Adam, and us his Eve, the stronger and weaker vessel, redeemed by the precious blood of our Lord, Jesus Christ.

Nation of Sex

We Americans live in a wicked nation. There is no worldly place or person we can look to that isn't oppressed by a spirit of lust for the pleasures of the world — the capitalist's dream and the materialist's joy. With discerning eyes, it is impossible not to acknowledge the sexualization of America, both literally and metaphorically.

Oh, America, you filthy nation, you have been perverted by the powers that be, bearing daughters in your image and raising them in the same manner. You are a nation of sex. The men you produce are of that nation, and the women you create complement that notion. It has become impossible to separate your salesmanship from your product, for this nation has adopted the philosophies of its marketers who have departed from their upbringing and become synonymous with their distribution. Every icon, pop star, influence, and even ordinary citizen who walks the streets is nothing short of objectification, convincing us that the flesh is far more desirable than the One who made it.

This is the symbol of America: Jezebel, the Idolater. We mirror our mother, spoken of in Christ's revelatory book. I expect this from American men and women, but I would least expect it from the men and women of God. As I examine the church of America, I see fewer and fewer believers in the image of God and, instead, in the American-made image of its master, the Devil. I recognize this is a controversial topic, primarily because of the principalities attached to those who have willfully attached themselves to them. Upon revealing it scripturally and spiritually, it will bite back with reasoning, gaslighting, and generally blinding its host, who aligns with it.

If you find yourself reasoning away our true modesty, I encourage you to check your spirit, for you do not engage your faith in this act, and instead instill your unbelief and disobedience, it will have dire consequences:

> I desire then that in every place the men should pray, lifting holy hands without anger or quarreling; likewise also that women should adorn themselves in respectable apparel, with modesty and self-control, not with braided hair and gold or pearls or costly attire, but with what is proper for women who profess godliness—with good works.
> — 1 Timothy 2:8-10 (ESV)

When God says to dress modestly, it is not up to our interpretation of what modesty is. Modesty, by definition and revelation, is orderly and of good behavior. Therefore, when examining the actions of the believers and the outward appearance of the group, we will either see the obedience God demands, the mistreatment of His word, or the contrary. In all, the fruit of our faith shall be made manifest in works, the completion and vindication of a true believer, who does not lust after the offerings of the world but the eternal security of our souls. Again, the eternal preservation of the saints is made real when we see the evidence of our justifying faith, so we may know what God has judged: eternally secure with life everlasting.

We should not shave our heads in disgrace to our Husband (1 Corinthians 11:5-6), meaning we should not be disobedient to what God has said, even if it means we give up some of our freedoms we most certainly have in Christ. All things are permissible, but not all things are profitable (1 Corinthians 10:23), and so in understanding this principle, we must have wisdom as to how we approach our walk with Christ mentally, emotionally, physically, and spiritually.

If pants are culturally rebellious or over-sexualized, perhaps we should not wear them; we should also not be fools to believe that to be over-sexualized is to wear pants. What is expressed upon ourselves outside is a reflection of what work is going on inside, and that is our evidence before men as to what is actual — a vindication of our faith. As we've established, the man, the husband, is the head, the pastor of his home, who provides for his family, and is the "working man." Though much more could be said on this topic, I encourage you to read the more extensive exegetical argumentation in the letter *"Garments of a Man"* in the text *American Made: Volume II*. What I aim to emphasize allegorically is that our American hearts should not be set on the matters of materialism, but on things of salvation. We should not claim to be a representative of Christ when, in actuality, we are better depicting our mother, America, who normalizes cross-dressing, sexual deviancy, and the rat race with no reconciliation.

I often wonder what the intention of the man or woman who wears revealing clothing is — one who seeks attention from their fellowman, perhaps in lustful ways, when we should only want the attention of Jesus. I have seen many Christian-claiming men revealing their upper bodies the same way that some women reveal everything but their most private places in dresses, jeans, or shorts. When leaving little to the imagination, we not only tempt our fellow Man, both male and female, unto sin, but sin ourselves when acting outside of the modesty requirement that God has put in place.

In America, lust for fame and fortune is the ultimate motivation we seem to struggle with, willing to sell out and prostitute ourselves for the sake of whichever idol — false god we serve. We have little to no respect for ourselves, that we would sell our bodies, even our souls, for five seconds of fame on an app of vanity, a shot at the big time, or even just the attention of people we don't know. I find social media to be like a drug, a harsh one, that, though at first seems like it's controllable, harmless, and fun, becomes a slave master that runs your life. It is like cocaine, only this drug is deceptively normalized, though it is a gateway to pornographic egoism. We thrive on lust, envy, jealousy, and vanity, and those who are eventually overcome by their temptation.

Worst of all, we are rewarded for our bad behavior.

We are rewarded with attention, false vindication, fame, and fortune. With this motivator, we slowly strip away their morals and biblical foundation, sometimes with our clothing more than that of the average stripper, only now, a local club isn't needed. Now, we have a global burlesque that many in the Christian community dance in, disgracing the testimony of Christ by displaying a false representation of it.

We fornicate with the world when we should be looking out for its consequences.

Modest apparel reveals nothing, for it is worn in shamefacedness, meaning it is "done in shame." The word "shamefaced" is associated with rhetoric such as humility, discomfort, and embarrassment. There is *nothing* shamefaced or humble about intentionally exposing yourself, drawing attention to yourself through the sexualization of your body. There is also nothing good about watching it and engaging with the behavior.

In other words, a fruit of the spirit is self-control, and that goes both ways in this circumstance (Galatians 5:22-23).

Now, the scriptures state that a man who lusts after a woman is held responsible for his lust (Matthew 5:28). Therefore, in principle, we must have self-control despite someone else's lack of it, if that is even the contextual reason for the behavior. We should be praying instead of lusting; we should certainly not be wrathful because of others' bad behavior (as we perceive it), and the non-interest those people may have in us. We should not doubt the Word and command that God has given to us, for then we are immodest. To put it differently, a parent is responsible for their son's and daughter's anger when they provoke it, but it is we who must control our anger if we are provoked. Thus, in all this, we see the checks and balances and the importance of recognizing how our actions can and will affect ourselves and others.

If we have no shame, we will have consequences for that lack of it, at least for those sons and daughters of God who desire correction.

If we are going to preach the Gospel, we should do it shamefacedly, behaving as a Christian behaves and not like the American-made one. What a terrible thing: to witness such a decimation of the church of Christ in America due to the false fellowship with her false gods. These spirits are not only lustful but also partake in defensive methods of manipulation, attempting to gaslight individuals such as myself when corrections are made. They have a clever means of using fear and blame shifting onto the judge, claiming that the criticism is only drawn by a perverse and lust-filled person rather than by biblical principles.

To that, I say, "I am not a lust-filled man, but a Holy Ghost-filled one. I do not fear your spirit. The only One I fear is the Lord." That is why I speak *boldly* on such matters, not to your offense alone, but to your aid, to wipe away the fog of deceit that blinds you. I hope you see that by drawing criticism to both genders, I do not look to one or the other when drawing attention to deception, but examine both sides of the church, especially when looking at the men and women who claim to live a life of Christ, yet do not do it expressly.

We should be clothed in righteousness. How can you say that is so when your character, which is reflected in your outward expression, is more reflective of Jezebel than Jesus? You act like an idolatrous murderer, trying to get people's attention, playing to your vanity and pride while getting drunk off the blood of the saints, the lustful attention of fleshy minds who pull you into contrary doctrines. You desire to be worshipped, to play God, and reject and revile His people, refusing the warnings that come to you, sooner desiring the execution of God's people than embracing the execution of our flesh.

There is only one end for a character who does such things: It is brutally described as someone who is thrown out of a tower, splats onto the ground, and becomes dog food consumed, digested, and excreted across the fields as dung, leaving only the unclean hands as a remnant. This was Jezebel, and though this graphic end may not be physically applicable today, it is parabolically. This end will come again. It has been prophesied. That same vain, sexual, finely-adorned world church will rise with the antichrist, whose spirit has already come and can be seen in those who twist the Word of God, producing an unclean temple that is akin to the one Christ turned the tables inside of upon seeing what the Jews had done to it: used it to sell, barter, trade, and gamble as opposed to worshipping God, as they were commanded to.

I pray you understand now why I am writing this. It is not to attack you but to show you the *danger* of your lifestyle. You *must* represent the Gospel correctly. Brothers and sisters, your bodies are sacred, and in keeping the laws of the Lord, you sanctify them daily.

Some sacrifices must be more tremendous than others. I understand this. The good news is that with every sacrifice, there is a proportionate blessing. Therefore, we can make excuses or sacrifices; depending on our choice, we will bring a blessing or a curse upon ourselves. There's nothing wrong with wanting to spread the Gospel, but we must do it in Spirit and Truth — in the Spirit of God and according to His Word. I don't believe it's hard to see how *sly* the Devil can be with his twisting of it, saying, "Modesty is subjective." Nothing that God says is subjective. It is an objective truth, and this objective truth, down to its root, is: "of good behavior" and "orderly." By definition, it is "the quality of being unassuming or moderate in the estimation of one's abilities," which are not *our* abilities, but God's. He is within us when we are *one* with *Him*, and so, with the Holy Spirit having sealed us, our hearts are made more humble every day.

"Unassuming" means humble, meek, mild, reserved, not bold, boastful, or pretentious. By another definition, we see modesty as "behavior, manner, or appearance intended to avoid impropriety or indecency." Impropriety means misconduct, dishonesty, corruption, transgression, and trespass, while indecency means obscenity, rudeness, crudity, and wickedness — a pornographic image.

I hope you see now.

There is a saying that goes, "Sex sells." This is an incredibly poignant and reflective phrase for America. It was made to describe an image produced by *Pearl Tobacco Company*, which had released a portrait of the goddess Venus, depicted naked, to advertise their cigarettes. This goddess symbolizes love, beauty, sex, fertility, and victory.

Examine Venus, who exemplifies love for the world, the beauty of sin, the fertility of the soul impregnated by its sinful desires, and the victory of the enemy, present in a Roman goddess, no less. I find it no coincidence that this American company that desires to sell items that destroy the body, leading many to a cancerous death, would use such a means of advertisement. It mirrors its nation, which is a copy of its predecessor, Rome. Only, now, it is the Gentiles and not the Jews that reject Christ, accepting Pagan gods while fornicating with their Roman mother under the guise of many names. As a believer, there is nothing more grievous than seeing a Christian claim to represent Christ and instead act like his enemy. I pray that one day you see this and determine that you would much rather align yourselves with the truth of the Kingdom of God than the philosophies of a cigarette company.

Those whose bodies the blood of Jesus Christ has purchased know they are not for sale. They know this by revelation, believing we give ourselves to him entirely, making him our Lord. May you accept the pardon for your redemption, and go forward doing good things for our precious Lord God, as evidence of a justified individual who is held forever in the Father's and Son's hand.

Apologetics

M y fellow Americans,

Amid a world of darkness with its children inhabiting, coming into the world speaking lies and continuing to do so, I greet thee in the name of the Lord Jesus Christ. This letter is meant to clarify rather than combat. I know that in the letters previous to this and the ones that will proceed it, I have come against many confusions, dogmas, false doctrines, and lies, which have put me in the proverbial hot seat or, at the very least, forced me to walk through a hall of critics that will come to hate the through line of justification. This Jamesian foundation explores the vindication of the American Christian.

Today, however, I have one goal that I hope will not spark so much controversy: to clarify a minor detail in our precious Word. I am not here to be combative, contrarian, or different, but to aid us all in our unified battle against the enemy, the Devil:

> Now who is there to harm you if you are zealous for what is good? But even if you should suffer for righteousness' sake, you will be blessed. Have no fear of them, nor be troubled, but in your hearts honor Christ

the Lord as holy, always being prepared to make a defense to anyone who asks you for a reason for the hope that is in you; yet do it with gentleness and respect, having a good conscience, so that, when you are slandered, those who revile your good behavior in Christ may be put to shame. For it is better to suffer for doing good, if that should be God's will, than for doing evil.
— 1 Peter 3:13-17 (ESV)

I have been found guilty of suffering for doing evil. This is a laughable mistake, in my opinion, for it is of no profit to me that I should welcome the evildoer's evil, nor do good by unrighteous means despite my own justification for them. I, along with many Christian apologists, have come to find that we often fail far more than we succeed when it comes to holding our own against egotistical, demon-oppressed, or generally detestable people. So, much like them, I look at the famous and influential script in 1 Peter, and use it to get myself into arguments or to prove myself or the scripture on a public platform. The error, here, is in being more interested in winning an intellectual argument for our own pride than in winning a soul for Christ. We will use His Word to vaunt ourselves up, without being humble enough to realize that the goal is not victory or even conversion, but sharing the truth — a defense for the hope that is in us. This is the mission of the apologist, and one that I believe is often overlooked.

We are more gardeners than arguers, and to have the expectation that the seed will not always take when planting in harsh conditions is a healthy and wise one to have. There are different types of soil hearts. Most of those we evangelize will not hear us. This has been my experience with everyone who has been deceived: Roman catholics, atheists, Message believers (and like cultists), even my fellow Protestants: their hearts are hardened and their hubris mighty.

One might think, *What good is an answer given, a defense made if they are not even asking to hear it?*

An answer is a thing written or said in reaction to a question in a test or quiz, the correct solution to a question in a test or quiz, a solution to a problem or dilemma, or a thing or person that *imitates* or *fulfills* the same role as *something* or *someone* else. In the King James Version, this word is used instead of "defense." They are transliterally the same, but possess slightly different connotations — angles to the same meaning. On the one hand, you have essentially provided the truth. On the other hand, you have the action of defending from or resisting an attack, or presenting a case by or on behalf of the party being accused. This is often central for Christianity; for 2000 years, it has been attacked by the embarrassing failure of every false doctrine, god, and atheist. This is primarily because of the apologist who, though I once believed were unnecessary, now understand are primarily central to our faith, in a most ironic fashion.

As it is, the second edition of this text is me defending Christianity from myself. Imagine the irony.

The Lord tests us often, usually by placing us in situations that require accountability of character and the wielding of the sword, as we best know how, at that time, to combat the enemy. We understand that the enemy is not the people but Satan, within, upon, and among them. With this in mind, we do not place the person as the adversary but as an inquiring mind. The test is given so that an *answer* found in the Word of God can be provided with proper fruit and evidence. Therefore, the solution is spiritual, not intellectual alone, for God's Word is understood by revelation which comes with both Spirit and Truth -- grace and law. Many people who come with questions, though having a negative attitude, do not come for wickedness's sake alone but because they have a *problem*: though they have an understanding, even a belief in heavenly places and supernatural concepts, they do not possess the key of knowledge needed to enter the pearly gates. Because of their lack of understanding, they are led to fear, which leads to doubt and the planting of a seed of hate. Thus, the demons with these souls bound have created a problem that only the eternal Word of God can solve, and that is where the apologist comes in.

Where is our grace when we respond to the lost? Where has our humbleness, respect, and good conscience gotten off to? I ask myself this question often. I try to justify my bad behavior by saying, "I have been dealing with hundreds of hateful comments. It's okay if my patience finally runs dry," to which I am convinced by the thought of, *What if the one it ran dry upon was the one who needed it the most?*

The lost, like we once were, have a dilemma, and we, being the children of God, have the solution. We are the people who represent Jesus Christ in his day, not taking his place but doing the works as his workmanship. We are not placed here to defend egos, but the Word of God, for our defense is the Word. So what if we are to be insulted, come upon hardships, persecutions, and calamities? Do not these weaknesses make us strong, meaning that our reliance on Christ's power is what makes grace abound when we are at our lowest — that there is purpose in the suffering when Christ is made visible in it (2 Corinthians 12:10).

What have we to be offended by the fools and the deceived, the arrogant and the ignorant? Let us give the good news so that those with an ear can hear and be convicted of contrition, so they may desire Jesus by faith and repent, so that they may be sealed by the Holy Spirit, producing a New Birth. This may not happen all in the same moment; that does not mean it will not happen at all:

> But do not overlook this one fact, beloved, that with the Lord one day is as a thousand years, and a thousand years as one day. The Lord is not slow to fulfill his promise as some count slowness, but is patient toward you, not wishing that any should perish, but that all should reach repentance.
> — 2 Peter 3:8-9 (ESV)

A defense can also be defending a title or a seat in a contest or election, and a military measure or resource for protecting a country. The King of Kings, the Lord Jesus Christ, has already won that title by conquering death, after which he ascended on high to sit at the right hand of God, making the contest no contest. He opened the way for the elect to step into their redeemed way of righteousness. Therefore, for those who are his sons and daughters, he is their defense against the principalities that plague us. He is the militaristic defense against Satan's legions, for he has sent us one who can teach us and bring to remembrance what we need (John 14:26), particularly when facing those who come against the holy country.

It is not us nor our intellect alone, but what God does within us; in our weaknesses, we are made strong.

Scripture forms this defense, the whole armor of God. With it, we must have our loins girt about us with the truth, wearing a breastplate of righteousness, and having our feet shod with the preparation of the gospel of peace. Above all, we should have the shield of faith and the helmet of salvation, paired with the sword of the Spirit, being the Word of God (Ephesians 6:11-18).

This is our defense, needing no man-made or self-inspired work to defend it to the people, but to be used as a spiritual defense of our hearts so that the enemy can stand in shame when they come against us. In fairness, I recognize that, in certain circumstances, some people come with *accusations* rather than questions, to which we look to another definition of the word answer: to defend oneself against a charge, accusation, or criticism. However, even *this* requires spiritual wisdom and should be sifted through, for they also accused Christ of not being the son of God before his crucifixion, and in response, he said nothing (Matthew 27:12-14). There are also instances in which the Pharisees combated Jesus with false doctrines (man-made legalism), and he appealed to Scripture to refute them (Matthew 23; Mark 7). Thus, when the accuser, the Devil, comes, we must discern whether we should be silent or provide a defense, and above all, retreat to our defense, which is Christ himself, remembering the objective of the conversation. If we are accused of lying because of the people's confusion, we answer with meekness, fear, and a good conscience. If we are asked to prove something or are asked questions in an effort to have our words twisted, prompting us to make a futile defense, then we would be wise to know that the inevitable truth of Christ will expose the fraud, and that silence is a wiser answer.

Sometimes, we are inclined to defend the Word because *they* have no spiritual defense. We falsely place our peace and sanctuary within our intellectualism — the need to show how smart we are. This is egotism and produces a false trust in our own hands more than in God's. Many Roman Catholics and Eastern Orthodox fall into this trap: They are wise fools who have read men's philosophies and determined that Man knows better than God. They are not unintelligent, but have become victims of it and are deceived by their hubris. I say all this to conclude on a simple note: Doing these things, as the scriptures state, will have a promised outcome to turn the evildoers who speak evil of us to shame. This is not to say that we will be exalted because of our argumentation, but in most cases brought low, often by the clowns who honk and holler at the Cirque des Circonciseurs.

A soul for Christ is not the apologist's prize; it is Christ's and the convert's, having him exalted in their lives, making him their Lord. Our reward is knowing that this has already happened for us, and that we are thankful to be a part of the process. The Word of God convicts us unto the contrition of change — the guilty heart to remorse, leading to a desired change of heart that, through faith, completes the justification process from then on, so that at *that point*, we may know that we have eternal life (1 John 5:13). Therefore, the goal is not to put people down or win a verbal joust but to lead them to the everlasting truth, letting the Lord plant the seed of life inside the lost so they can be saved at the time appointed to them (Ecclesiastes 3:1).

Let us have a good conversation in Christ, not a hateful debate. One cannot win a soul to the Lord through a game of wits without fruit, but through the life-giving Word that is knowledgeable, wise, and spirit-led. Though it may be hard to see, those who do evil works have the same souls as ours.

Love them at all costs with an eternal love unto their shame.

Whom Shall Be Saved

*F*or God so loved the world that He gave His only begotten Son, that whosoever believeth in Him shall not perish, but have eternal life. God didn't send his Son into the world to condemn it, but so that it could be saved through him (John 3:16-17).

Anyone who is a Christian knows these scriptures, and some even know them by heart. At any time, place, and from any mouth, these words, spoken or read, will ring to recognition in the ears and hearts of any believer, self-declared or not.

Still, few understand it.

I have even caught myself misinterpreting this text, connecting it to a similar scripture that the current Christian totes: "Go ye into all the world and preach the gospel." We know it is a great commission, but we miss the person for whom it was commissioned.

So, I ask: Whom shall be saved?

Aside from noting that John 3:16 clearly asserts that believers, after having faith, are saved, making the eternal preservation of the saints even more biblical, this commission led me to ask a further question: Is the commission sent to the world or to the believer? To answer this, we must first ask who is a believer: someone who believes but has not worked, or someone who has had a personal revelation of who Jesus Christ is, been changed, and works as a thankful expression of love because of that faith? How do we identify the evidence, justification, and vindication of the believer and determine their, even our, eternal destination?

I consider the worldly, the materialistic: God so loved the *world* that He gave His only begotten Son. Here are some of God's thoughts on the world:

> Paul says the world is not to be conformed to (Romans 12:2).
> John declares not to love it or its things (1 John 2:15).
> God promises that the world will hate Him and he who is of Him (John 15:18-19).
> James states that the friendship of the world is enmity with God (James 4:4).

All that is of the world is not of the Father, for he who is of the world is exclusively of the flesh, and not of the world to come, but chooses to remain in this one, which, as we know, is Satan's (2 Corinthians 4:4). There is more than one way to not belong to God but be fascinated by the things of this world — the things of men. All of it is by religion, whether that religion be theism, atheism, or cultism. It is hard to discern which is which in such an elusive world as ours, but more than anything, we should discern what is of "the world" and therefore what we should not partake in unwisely, living within it, being sent to *someone* inside it, like we are, and once were, more attributively. We are not sent to start emotion-based, charismatic revivals but to help regenerate the soul inside the foreordained saint. We find God's ordainment in the production of spiritual life. Anything outside of His ordainment will only produce death.

I see so much death these days.

The Holy Spirit does *nothing* for the people of this world and *everything* for the children of God, which is not someone who declares they are a Christian alone but has that Abrahamic seed (Genesis 15:5-6) within them, producing a work sometimes decades later that vindicates the justified person (Genesis 22:12). The people of this world do not know Christ, but their traditions and their materialism that they have replaced him with. They demonize the individual who proclaims their relationship over religion while simultaneously rejecting the relationship for their religion. Alas, some may be enlightened and taste of the things of God; that does not always mean they are saved (Hebrews 6:5). The saved, however, are more concerned about better things than the goodness of the Word of God, the powers of the age to come, and do not fall away knowing the things that belong to salvation (Hebrews 6:8), for if we were of the things that shrink back and are destroyed, we would not be of those who have faith and preserve our souls by it (Hebrews 10:39).

What the Hebrews lead us to conclude is that the rain falls on the wheat and the weeds, but only the wheat will be harvested, which is found in their seed, while the weeds will be caught up and burned due to their judgment (Matthew 13:24-30, 36-43). The wheat will have been planted by the farmer (the Son of Man) in the good soil. There are three types of soils (Matthew 13; Mark 4; Luke 8):

1. The hard soil, where the message is not understood, and the devil takes it away (the soil rejects it).
2. The thorny soil, where the message is choked by life's worries, riches, and pleasures (knew of God, but chose something other).
3. The good soil, where the message is heard, understood, accepted, and preserved by God, producing a fruitful and changed life (the true believer).

The three believers, recognizing that Christianity is more than good feelings, cultural clubs, or legalistic rigidity, but souls that are restored when the Spirit of God seeps through the body and spirit, regenerating a deep-rooted faith. That is how life is produced, like the fruit from the tree of life, which all can see. Water seeps through the soil, but it does the seed no good unless the farmer plants it first. This is to say that the Holy Spirit may fall upon many like a dove, but a revival will only take place when it touches the soul that was first placed by God, who was, is, and will be a portion of the infinite God. A revival is not evidence of God, but the life produced when the soul is restored is.

The original creation restored to and by the Creator is made possible by the blood of Jesus.

In the simplicity of the synonym "revival," we see this understanding. In it, we find the word "restoration," which is to be restored, reconciled back to God, though we live in a fallen state. Despite the Adamic Covenant, then the

Law, we now have our glorious covenant of grace, which is all because of the completed work of God. Though we were once dead in sin, we now live, having been radically changed, no longer the same. The wages of the sins of our flesh have been paid, and it was by that one sacrifice that cleanses us (1 John 1:7) and purifies our conscience from dead works from all sin (Hebrews 9:13-14).

Yes, many are called, but few are chosen; know of God but do not know God; are among the saved but are not saved.

Strait is the gate, and narrow is the way. There are many denominations, but one church. There are many in-between, even more entirely lost, but only a *few* true believers. There is much death, lies, and life paths, but only one Way, Truth, and Life. This is individually attained, and when the person does, they are regenerated and made the Bride of Jesus Christ. It is they who Christ will come back for, whose names are written in the Lamb's book of life that cannot be blotted out (Revelation 3:5).

Now that we know that the evidence of a regenerated individual is produced from the life put into an individual at the time of true faith in Jesus, we can extend the examination to the fruits previously mentioned, along with their tree: Love, joy, peace, long-suffering, gentleness, goodness, faith, meekness, and temperance. He who has all of these is a justified man before men, and he who has meekness shall inherit the Earth.

Which Earth will you be a part of? The current Earth? The new one? The Earth that the meek shall inherit is that same revelatory Earth that John described on the Isle of Patmos, that will be created along with the new Heaven. It will be this same world, regenerated also, the same as Heaven must be since sin originated within it, then was made manifest to our destruction in Eden's inhabitants' consequential disobedience.

In the same way that Hell was created for Lucifer, his angels, and anyone who follows him (Matthew 25:41; Revelation 20), a perfect earth was made for us. *There* is our Eden; *there* is our promised land.

I say that to say this: a soul for Christ is eternal, as is God. A soul separated from Christ is eternally separated also. We can either spend eternity in the presence of His love and joy or of His judgment and wrath. Though we were sent to this Earth, we will go to a new one if we are written in the book. Adam and Eve were in Eden, and then they were put out into this one. Therefore, for a true restoration to take place, we must all be returned. Who is "we"? The redeemed — those who have made Christ their Lord by *humbling* themselves before him, following his every law, command, and footstep, not for justification in the legal sense, but in the evidential sense that displays a saved individual's fruits — his evidence — those of us who have been born again and have the fruits and works to prove it.

Those are the ones that are sealed until the day of their redemption. Therefore, we are redeemed, but waiting to be redeemed.

God loved the world, not the worldliness of it, in the same way that God loves the sinner but not the sin he engages with. Because of his abhorrence for such things, the world will be cleansed by fire and made new (2 Peter 3:10-12), in the same way that the believer is by receiving the Holy Spirit, cleansing our unrighteous works but not losing our salvation (1 Corinthians 3:13-15).

All sinners will be taken with that old world, but the bride will rejoice in her new Jerusalem.

Whosoever believes in him shall not perish but *have* everlasting life.

Not everyone will choose to believe in God, despite the overwhelming evidence for Him. Others will reject His grace, believing that their works, their righteousness, are what determine their eternal life. That leads us back to the original question: Who is the great commission for? It is for the believer alone, who is not simply someone who is saved or truly believes, but is continually preserved by God for all eternity. The ones whom God hand-selected according to what He saw in His omniscience, omnipresence, and understanding of predestination? Once again, I beg you to understand that I do not write this writ to refuse the Great Commission but to correctly identify who it is for so that the evangelist might succeed. The conceptual or cultural Christian might be vindicated. We know that we have righteous judgment. This is not the same as being the Righteous Judge. We can tell right from wrong but cannot condemn, for condemnation is God's alone, while we are here on this Earth. Meaning that we go into the world and preach the Gospel to all creation (Mark 16:15-18). It is not to the end of starting revivals, growing our lodges, or proclaiming our false virtue before the masses, but to the expected end of the sons and daughters of God that can only attain such titles through a spiritual birth — an internal revival — a personal restoration, which is what Christ was given for and the Holy Spirit seals.

We go to the world to preach the Gospel, but only *His* sheep will hear it (John 10:25-30). When we water the field, we pay no mind to the wheat or weeds, but let the great Harvester burn the weeds and harvest the grain when He deems it time, as well as recognize it is He who also does the watering.

We do not save; Christ saves.

We are simply sprinklers that let the Holy Spirit take hold of whosoever will so they may attain the revelation of Jesus Christ, and by truly believing in Him, might confess their faith, repent, and have eternal life.

God desires that all be saved, to come to the knowledge of the truth (1 Timothy 2:3-4), but we know they *all* will not. A desire is not the same as a decree, and though that is unfortunate and grievous, it does not mean that fighting the good fight for those who will is not worth it. Let this letter not rob you of your zeal but enable you to direct it better, and more importantly, not let the enemy who impersonates such good things use it. It is essential to know your enemy as much as it is to know your ally; otherwise, you may sooner work for him than the Lord. We cannot outsmart the devil on his grounds, but beat him on God's. How do we know we are on God's? We answer three simple yet powerful questions:

Who is my Lord?
Why am I here?
What is my enteral destination?

The answers:

Jesus is my Lord.
I'm here to serve God.
My eternal destination is with God, safe and secure.

Knowing this, the devil cannot shake you. I pray this helps and encourages you and will better direct you in your walk with the Lord. That is my main intention, not only with this passage but with the entirety of this text. May you find yourself in Christ, in God, and in the word, you who believe in Him, and will not perish but have everlasting life.

The grace of our Lord Jesus Christ be with you all.
Amen.

John Anderson

John Anderson is an award-winning Christian poet, songwriter, playwright, novelist, and escapee from the Message cult of personality. He lives in North Carolina, enjoys nature, watching movies, and loves his wife and cats. For his ministry, he seeks to lead people to Jesus through biblical centrism, providing nuance and realism to the average person's walk with God through mixed media. Currently, he's working to expand into acting, delve deeper into theatrical writing, and contribute to the ongoing effort to combat Christian cultism in America.

Above all, he remains a storyteller.

VISIT JOHN ANDERSON ONLINE

linktr.ee/johnandersonbookworks

▶ johnandertube

❋ ◉ ♪ johnandersonauthor

BOOKS BY JOHN ANDERSON

POETRY
Parable
Song of Cedar (coming soon)
Curtains (coming soon)
Lights (coming soon)

FICTION
The Price of Salvation: An American Legend
The Price of Retribution: An American Tragedy
The Price of Revelation: An American End (coming soon)

RELIGION, SPIRITUALITY, AND PHILOSOPHY
American Made: Volume I
American Made: Volume II
American Made: Volume III (coming soon)

MEMOIR
El Perro Leal: A Loyalist's Story of Surviving the Message Cult
(coming soon)

CHILDREN'S BOOKS
Where the Oak and Flowers Dance (coming soon)

HOW TO FEED AN AUTHOR

Dearest Readers,

Thank you for taking the time to read this text and for your support. This is the fourth of many independently published texts I will be doing, and your support, though singular, is not in the least minuscule or devalued. To that end, I again come to you with another plea: to write a review of this book. Reviews are essential to this book's success and a game-changer in any small author's career.

I'd greatly appreciate it if you wrote an honest review on the website where you purchased this text, especially on Amazon and Goodreads. Even if you didn't buy it there, please head over and write one.
It matters and means a lot.

You can also share this book on social media, recommend it to friends and family, engage with the content online, subscribe to and follow the YouTube channel and other social media, create fan content, participate in discussions at your local book club, forum, or online discussion boards, and, of course, gift it as a recommendation to your local library or book club.

Once again, thank you all so much for your support,
and may God bless you.

—John

QUESTIONS FOR DISCUSSION

1. What does it mean to be "American Made," and in what ways might our culture be shaping our faith more than Scripture does? Where do you see cultural values (politics, success, sexuality, money, or comfort) quietly influencing how Christians live and think?

2. The book repeatedly distinguishes between *professing faith* and *possessing faith*. What biblical signs distinguish genuine faith from cultural or inherited Christianity?

3. If salvation is by grace through faith alone, why does Scripture still place such emphasis on obedience, holiness, and good works? How do these truths coexist without contradicting one another?

4. Several letters challenge political and cultural loyalties. How can Christians engage with the world without allowing political identity to replace Christian identity in Christ?

5. The book suggests that fear (of rejection, suffering, or loss) often keeps believers silent. What fears most commonly prevent Christians today from speaking or living boldly for Christ?

6. Many people today seek self-improvement, self-reinvention, or personal growth. How is becoming a *new creation in Christ* fundamentally different from these ideas?

7. The letters describe a world deeply shaped by sin, yet still loved by God. How should Christians balance truth and compassion when confronting cultural sin?

8. The book warns about both spiritual isolation and blind loyalty to institutions. What does a healthy, biblical view of the church look like in practice?

9. Several chapters emphasize the Holy Spirit's work. What role should the Holy Spirit play in the daily life of a believer, and how can Christians become more dependent on Him?

10. Ultimately, the book asks a personal question: *Who truly belongs to Christ?* What does it mean to know Christ (not merely know about Him) truly, and how can a person examine their own heart honestly before God?

Final Reflection: Which letter in this book challenged or convicted you the most, and why?

John Anderson

"But when the goodness and loving kindness of God our Savior appeared, he saved us, not because of works done by us in righteousness, but according to his own mercy, by the washing of regeneration and renewal of the Holy Spirit, whom he poured out on us richly through Jesus Christ our Savior, so that being justified by his grace we might become heirs according to the hope of eternal life."

— Titus 3:4-7 (ESV)

www.ingramcontent.com/pod-product-compliance
Lightning Source LLC
Chambersburg PA
CBHW031257110426
42743CB00040B/724